# The Best of Popular Wedding Music

Piano/Vocal/Chords

Copyright © 1990 CPP/Belwin, Inc.
15800 N.W. 48th Avenue, Miami, FL 33014

Photo: © Maria Taglienti, THE IMAGE BANK
Editor: Carol Cuellar
Layout: Leyla Arner

WARNING: Any duplication, adaptation or arrangement of the compositions contained in this collection, without the written consent of the owner is an infringement of U.S. copyright law and subject to the penalties and liabilities provided therein.

# TABLE OF CONTENTS

| | |
|---|---|
| After All (Love Theme From "Chances Are") | 10 |
| All I Ever Need Is You | 162 |
| Always | 3 |
| Always and Forever | 151 |
| An Affair To Remember | 48 |
| And I Love You So | 98 |
| Ave Maria (Bach/Gounod) | 40 |
| Ave Maria (Schubert) | 101 |
| Bridal Chorus (From "Lohengrin") | 44 |
| Colour My World | 108 |
| Devoted To You | 38 |
| Feelings(¿Dime?) | 84 |
| For Me And My Gal | 118 |
| For Once In My Life | 66 |
| Forever And Ever, Amen | 80 |
| Glory Of Love (Theme From The Karate Kid Part II) | 142 |
| The Greatest Love Of All | 33 |
| Heaven | 62 |
| Here And Now | 6 |
| I Can't Stop Loving You | 116 |
| I Honestly Love You | 58 |
| I Just Called To Say I Love You | 157 |
| I Will Always Love You | 96 |
| I'd Fall In Love Tonight | 171 |
| If You Say My Eyes Are Beautiful | 92 |
| (Where Do I Begin) Love Story | 148 |
| My Only Love | 174 |
| Nobody Loves Me Like You Do | 18 |
| Now And Forever (You And Me) | 154 |
| On The Wings Of Love | 110 |
| One In A Million You | 89 |
| The Shadow Of Your Smile | 146 |
| Theme From Ice Castles (Through The Eyes Of Love) | 69 |
| (I've Had) The Time Of My Life | 72 |
| To Me | 120 |
| Tonight I Celebrate My Love | 26 |
| Up Where We Belong | 54 |
| The Vows Go Unbroken (Always True To You) | 15 |
| The Way You Do The Things You Do | 78 |
| Wedding March | 76 |
| We've Only Just Begun | 177 |
| What Are You Doing The Rest Of Your Life? | 136 |
| With You I'm Born Again | 165 |
| You And I | 50 |
| You And I | 23 |
| You And Me Against The World | 123 |
| You Are So Beautiful | 128 |
| You Are The Sunshine Of My Life | 168 |
| You Light Up My Life | 30 |
| You're The Inspiration | 131 |
| You've Made Me So Very Happy | 139 |

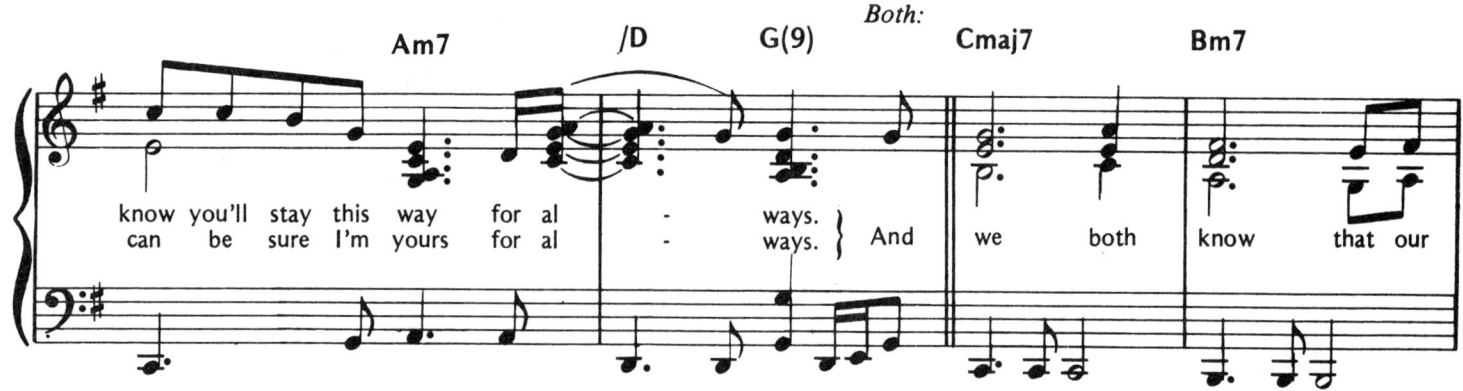
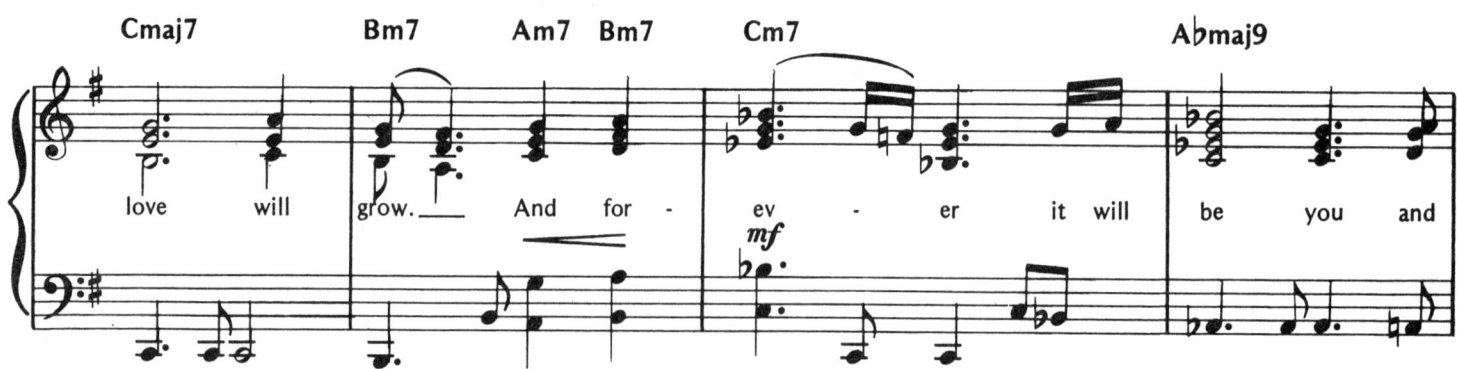

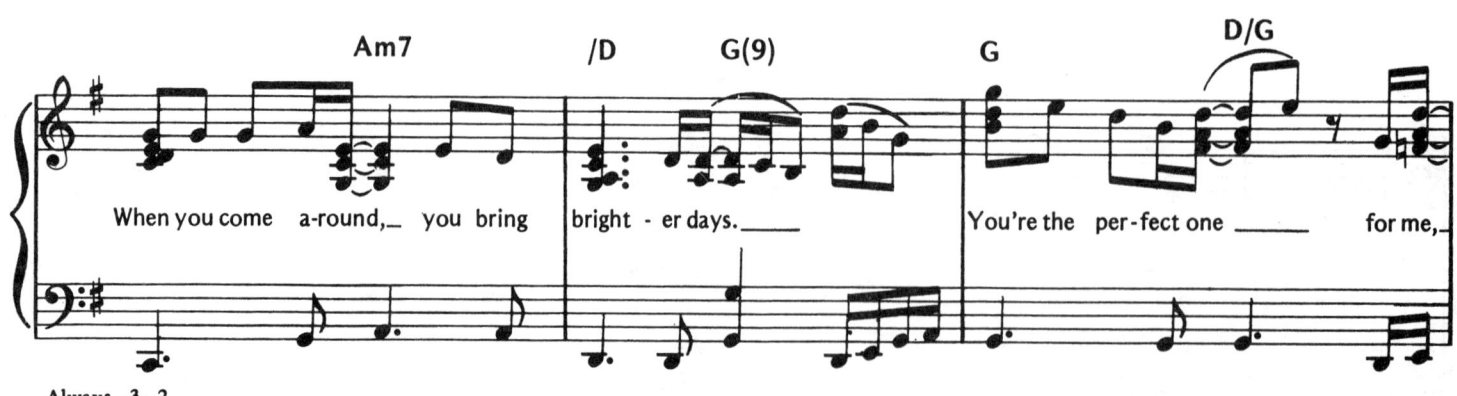

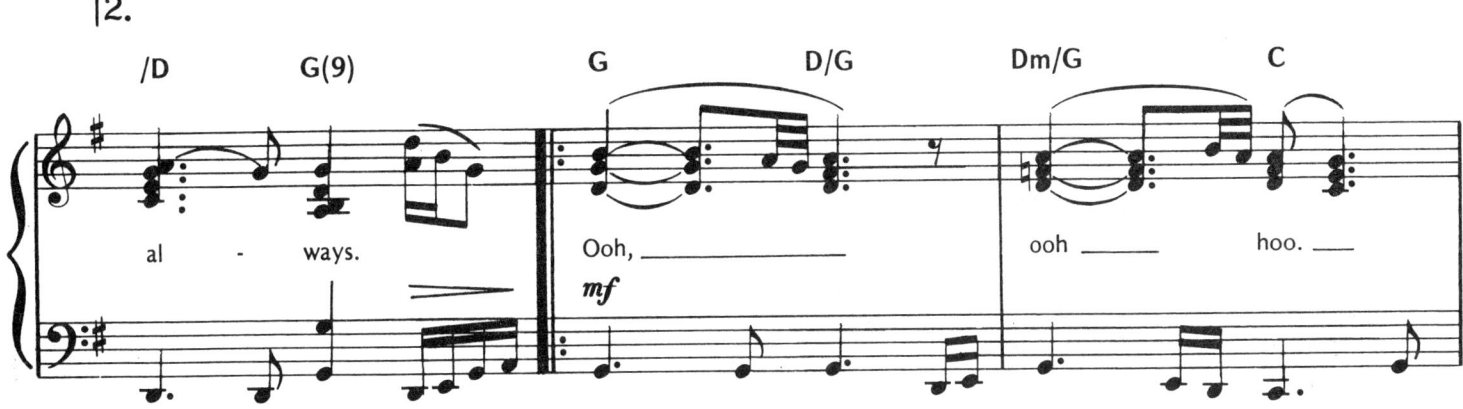

# HERE AND NOW

Words and Music by
TERRY STEELE and
DAVID ELLIOTT

Here And Now - 4 - 1

Copyright © 1989 DLE MUSIC/OLLIE BROWN SUGAR MUSIC
International Copyright Secured   Made In U.S.A.   All Rights Reserved

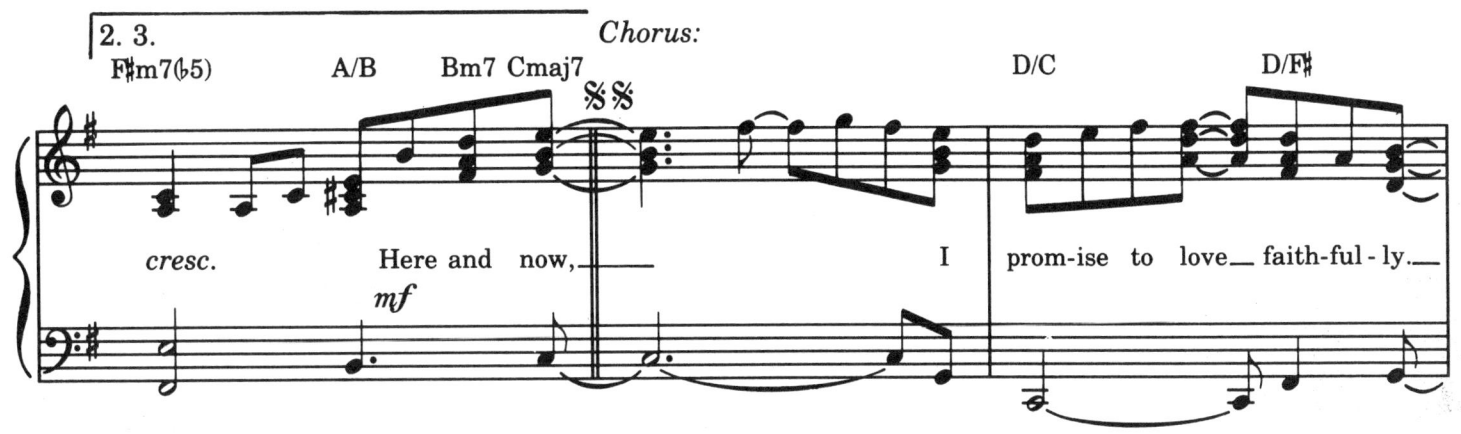

8

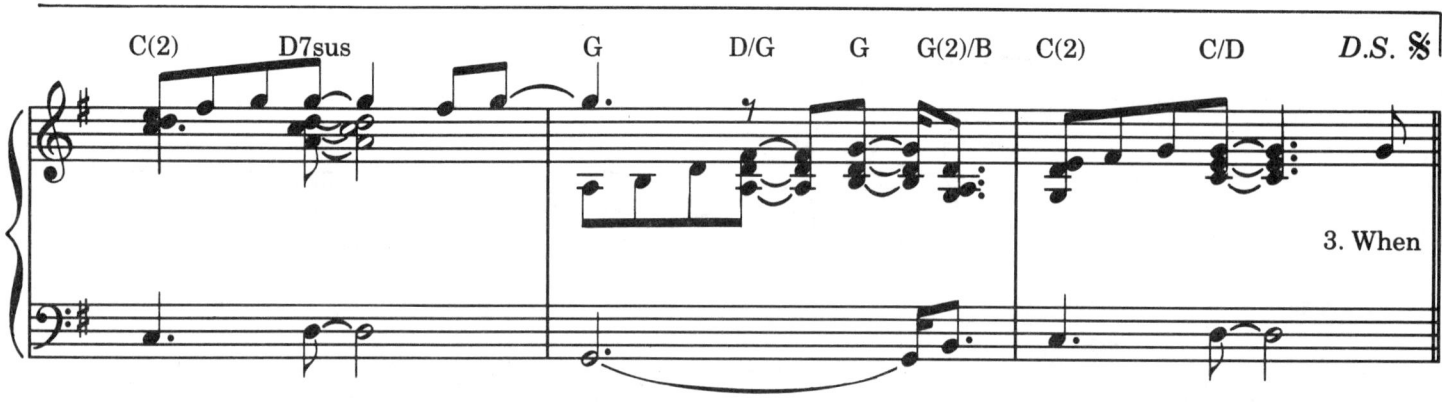
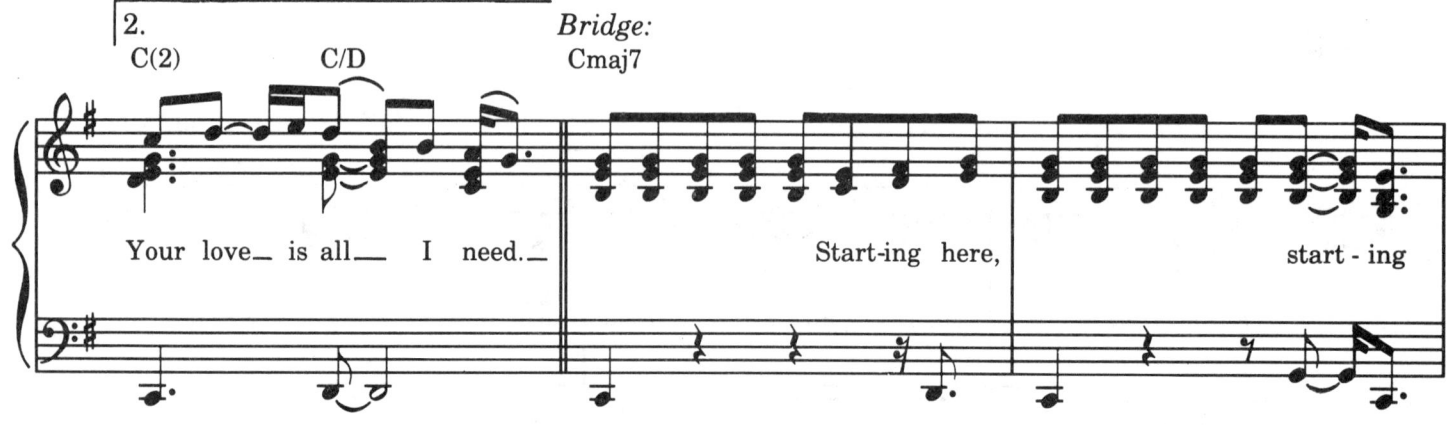

Here And Now - 4 - 3

*Verse 2:*
I look in your eyes and there I see
What happiness really means.
The love that we share makes life so sweet,
Together we'll always be.
This pledge of love feels so right,
And ooh, I need you.
*To Chorus:*

*Verse 3:*
When I look in your eyes, there I see
All that a love should really be.
And I need you more and more each day,
Nothing can take your love away.
More than I dare to dream,
I need you.
*To Chorus:*

From The Tri-Star Pictures film "CHANCES ARE"

# AFTER ALL
(Love Theme From "Chances Are")

Words and Music by
DEAN PITCHFORD and
TOM SNOW

*He:* 1. Well, here we are again;

Verse 1:

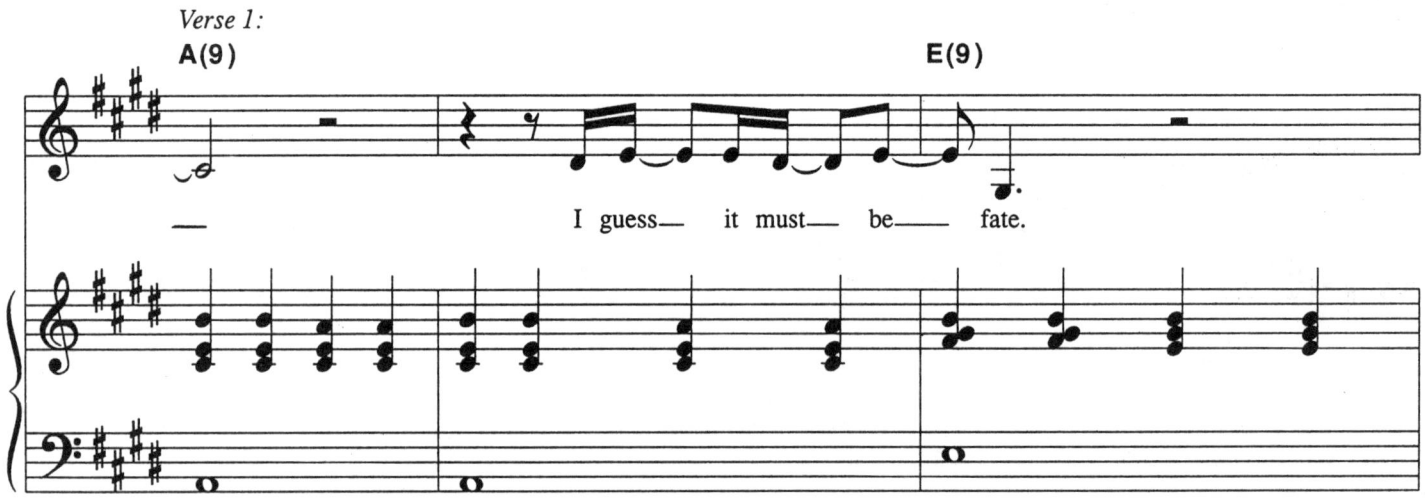

I guess it must be fate.

We've tried it on our own, but deep inside we've known we'd be back to set things

After All - 5 - 1

Copyright © 1989 TRIPLE STAR MUSIC, INC./SNOW MUSIC/PITCHFORD MUSIC
International Copyright Secured     Made In U.S.A.     All Rights Reserved

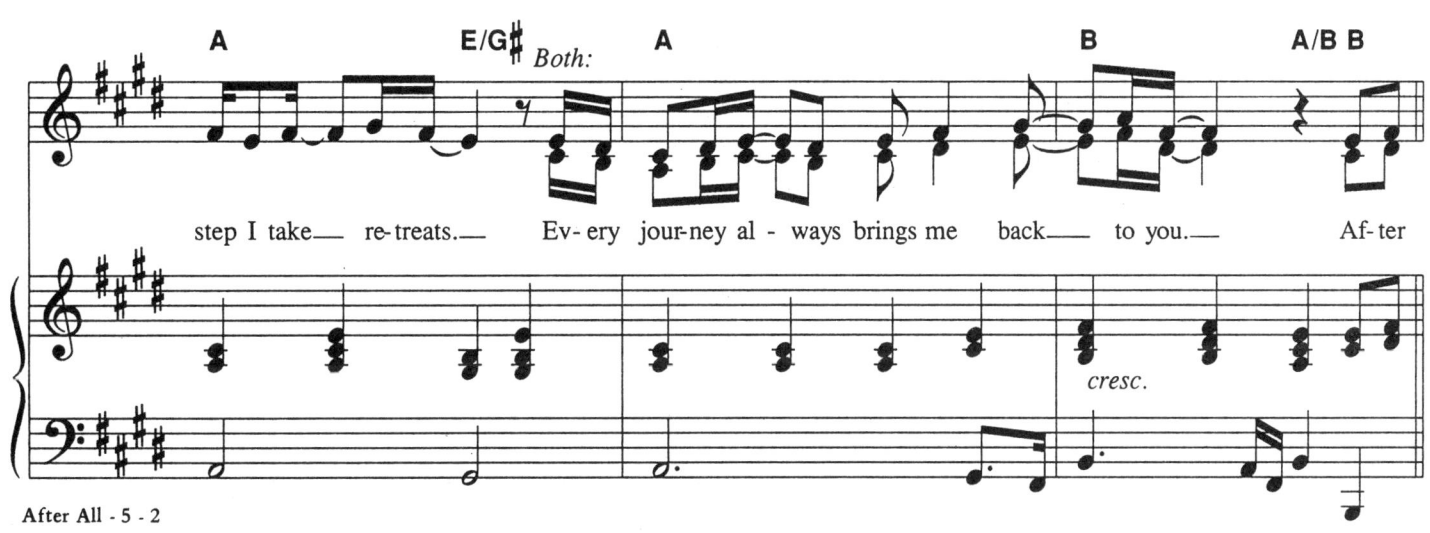

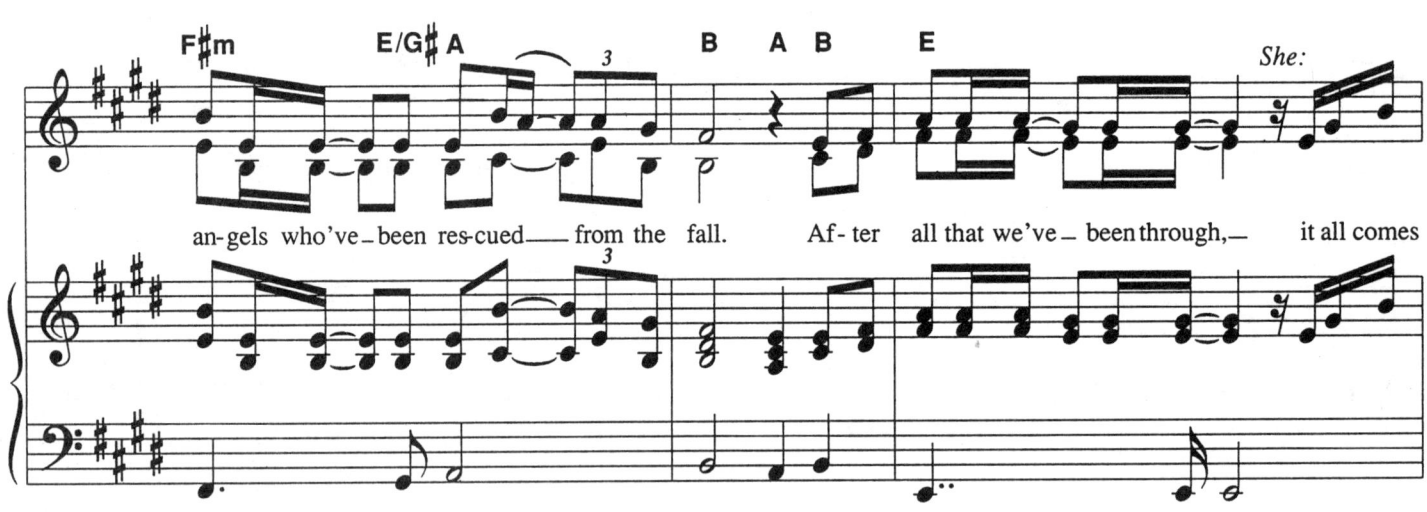

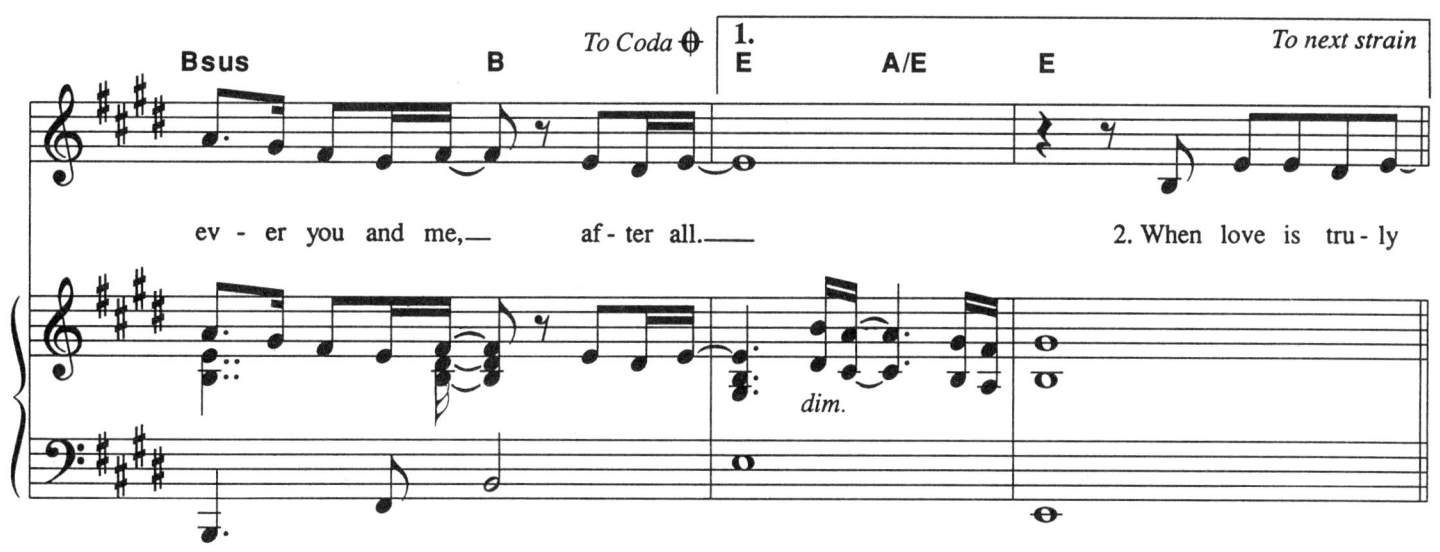
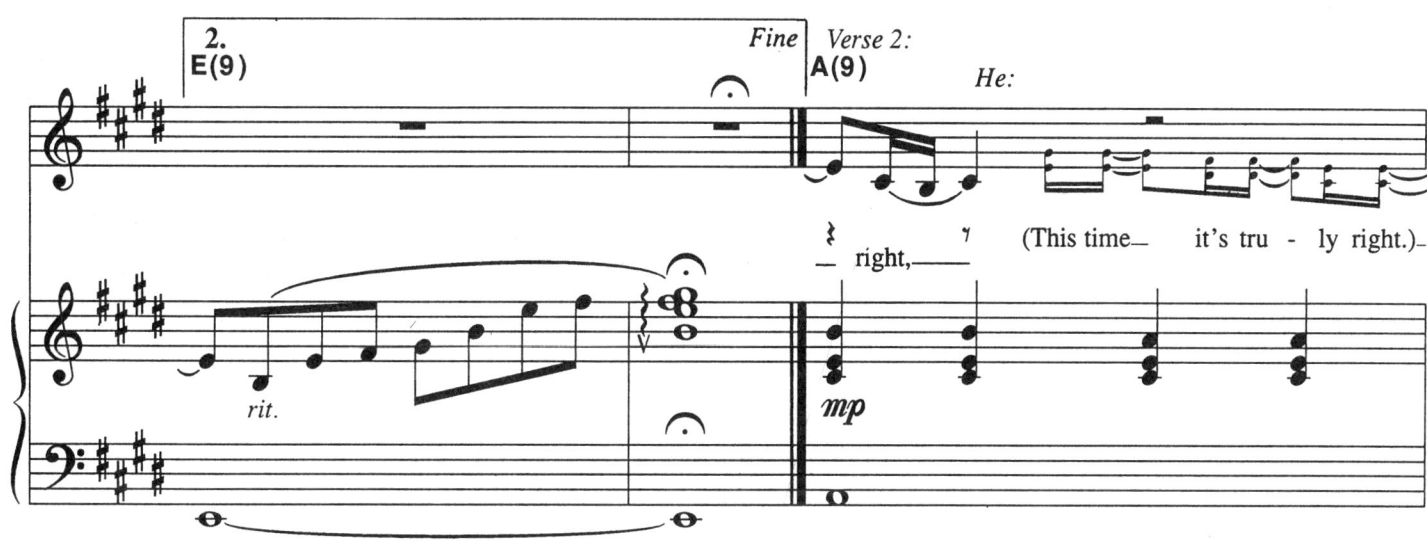
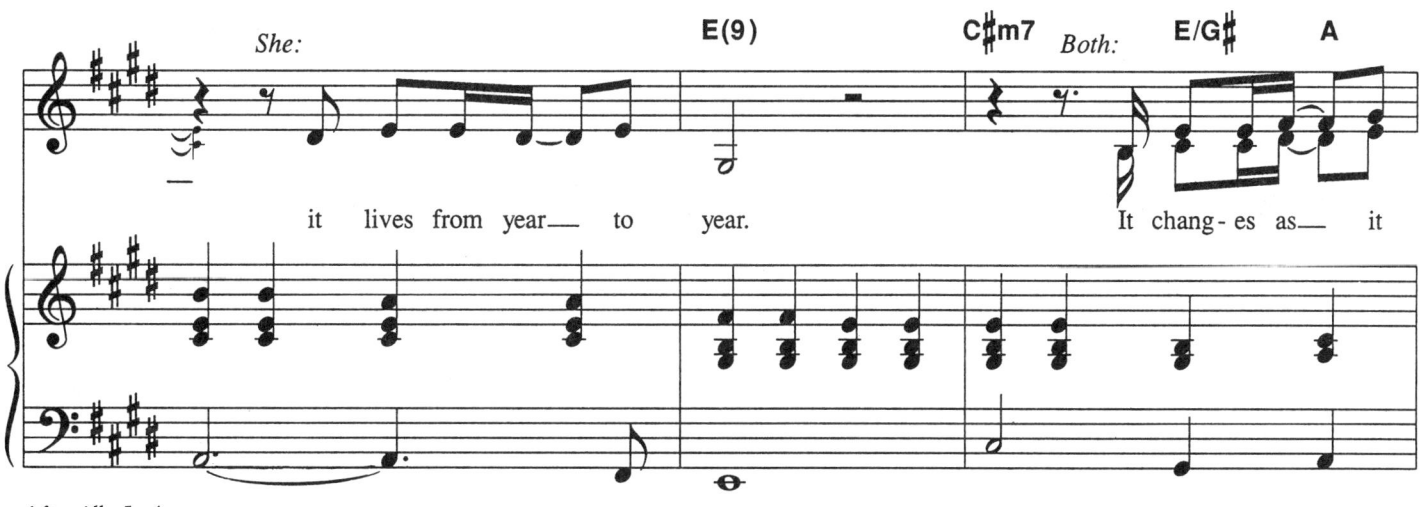

After All - 5 - 4

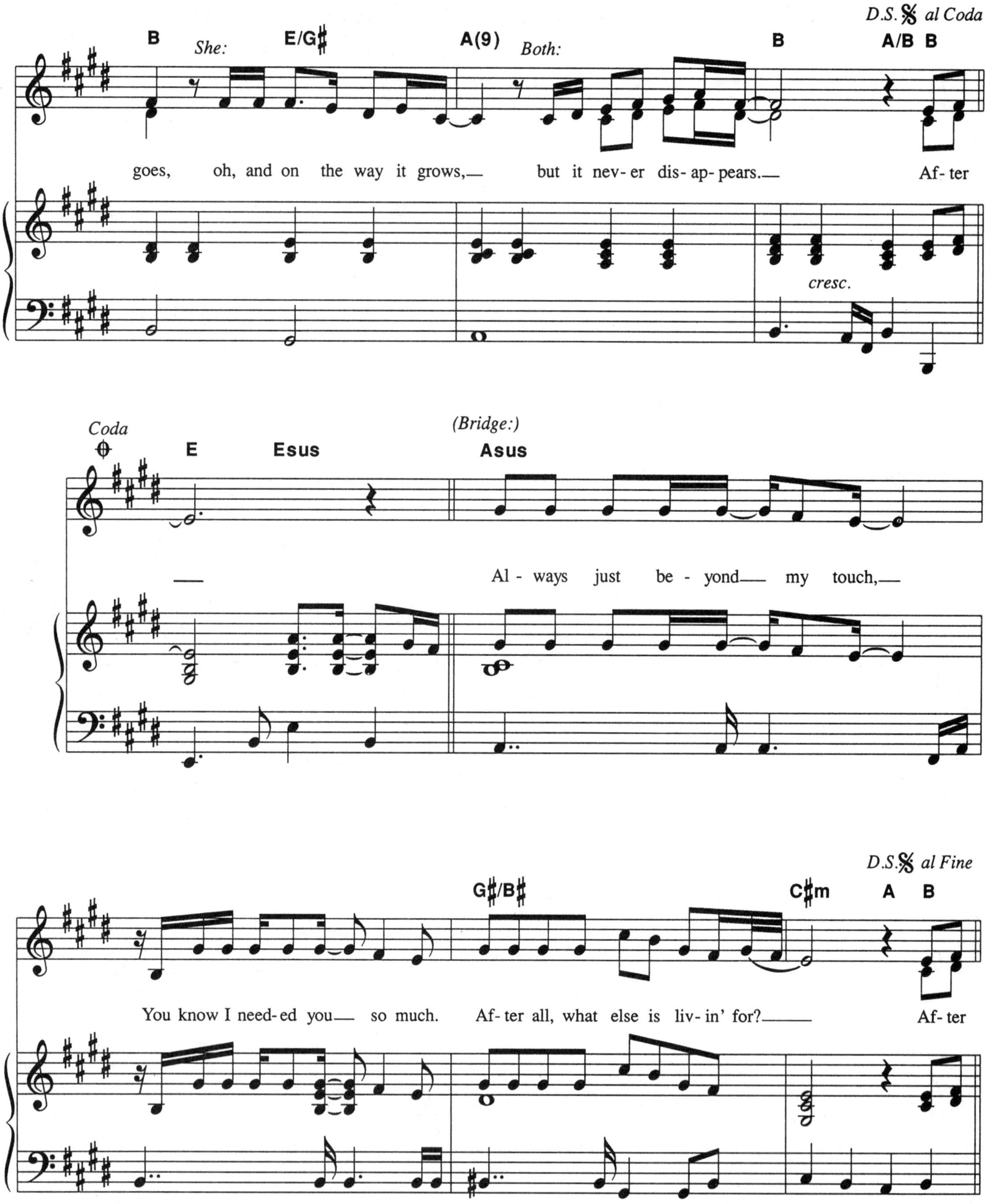
D.S. 𝄋 al Coda
B
She:
E/G♯
A(9)
Both:
B
A/B B
goes, oh, and on the way it grows,— but it nev- er dis- ap- pears.— Af- ter
cresc.
Coda
E
Esus
(Bridge:)
Asus
— Al - ways just be - yond— my touch,—
D.S. 𝄋 al Fine
G♯/B♯
C♯m
A B
You know I need- ed you— so much. Af- ter all, what else is liv- in' for?—— Af- ter

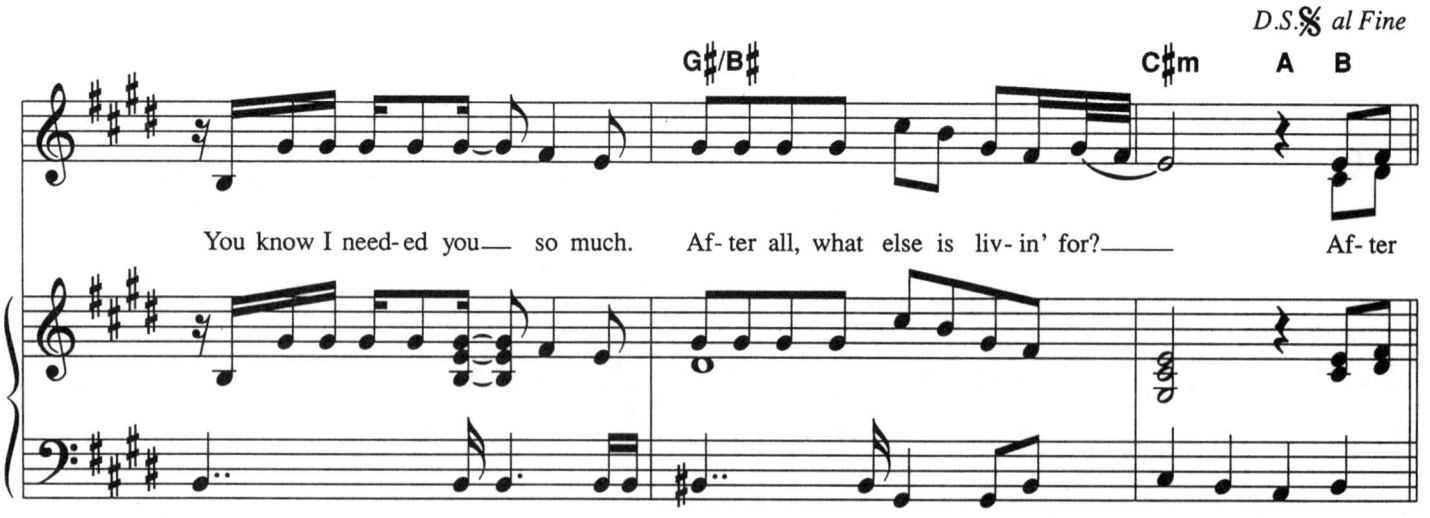

16

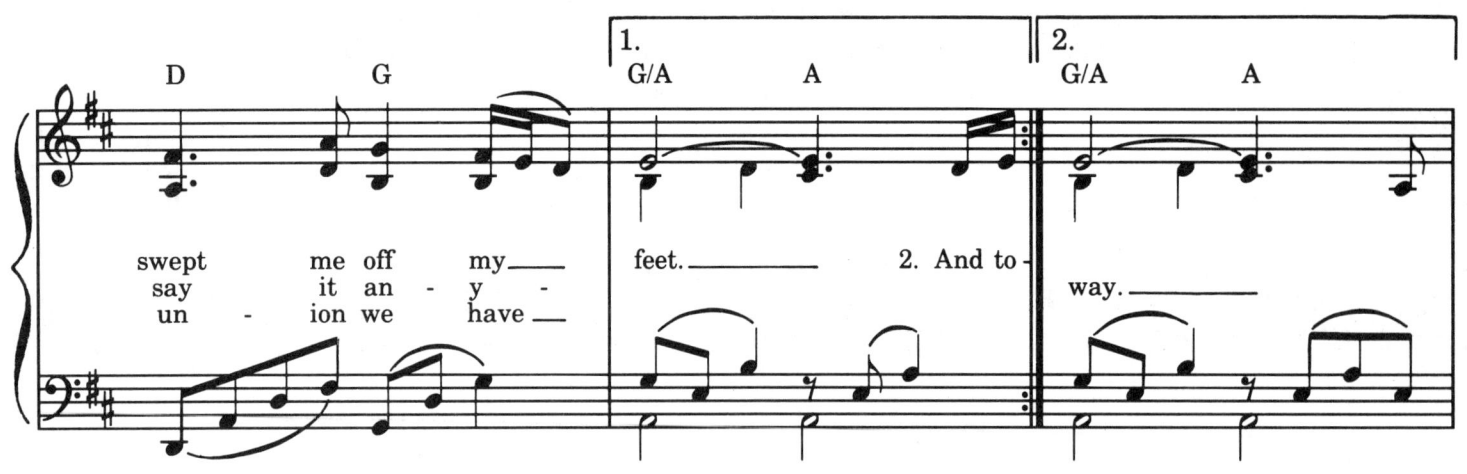
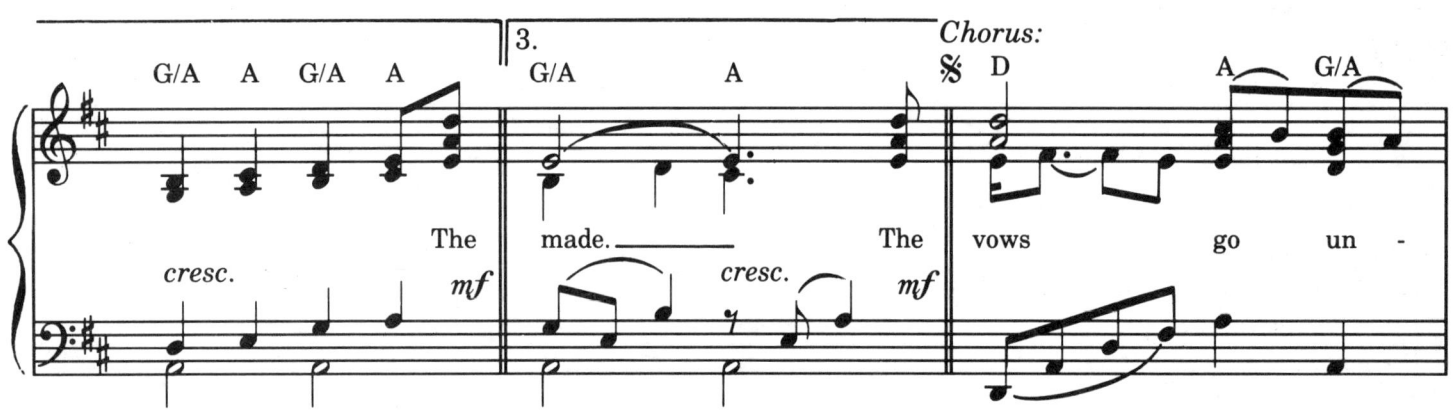

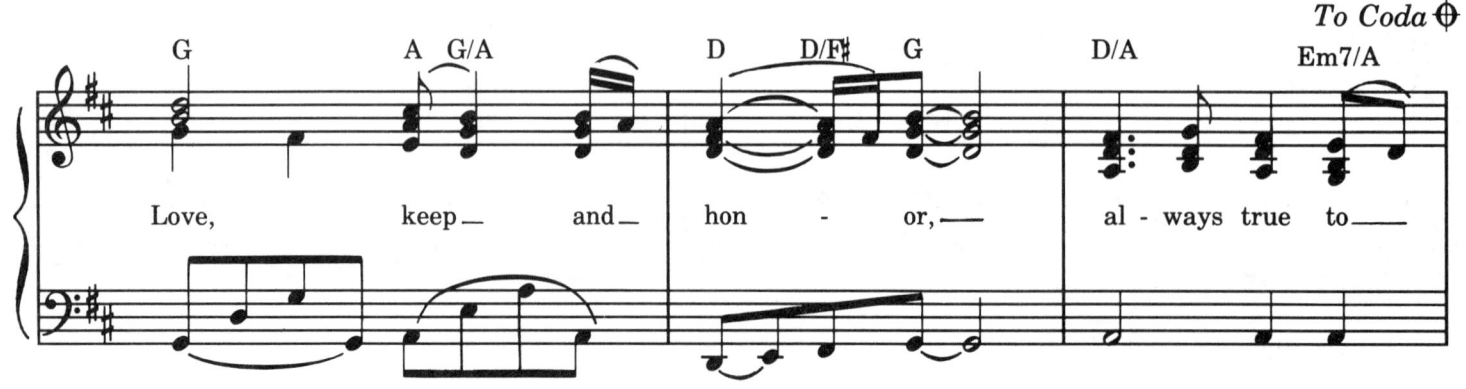

The Vows Go Unbroken - 3 - 2

Nobody Loves Me Like You Do - 5 - 4

**𝄋 3rd Verse:**

Boy: I was words without a tune,
Girl: I was a song still unsung.
Boy: A poem with no rhyme;
Girl: A dancer out of time;
Both: But now there's you.
Nobody loves me like you do.

*(To Chorus:)*

# TONIGHT I CELEBRATE MY LOVE

By MICHAEL MASSER and GERRY GOFFIN

Tonight I Celebrate My Love - 4 - 1

Copyright © 1983 SCREEN GEMS-EMI MUSIC INC., ALMO MUSIC CORP. and PRINCE STREET MUSIC
All rights administered by SCREEN GEMS-EMI MUSIC INC. and ALMO MUSIC CORP.
International Copyright Secured    Made In U.S.A.    All Rights Reserved

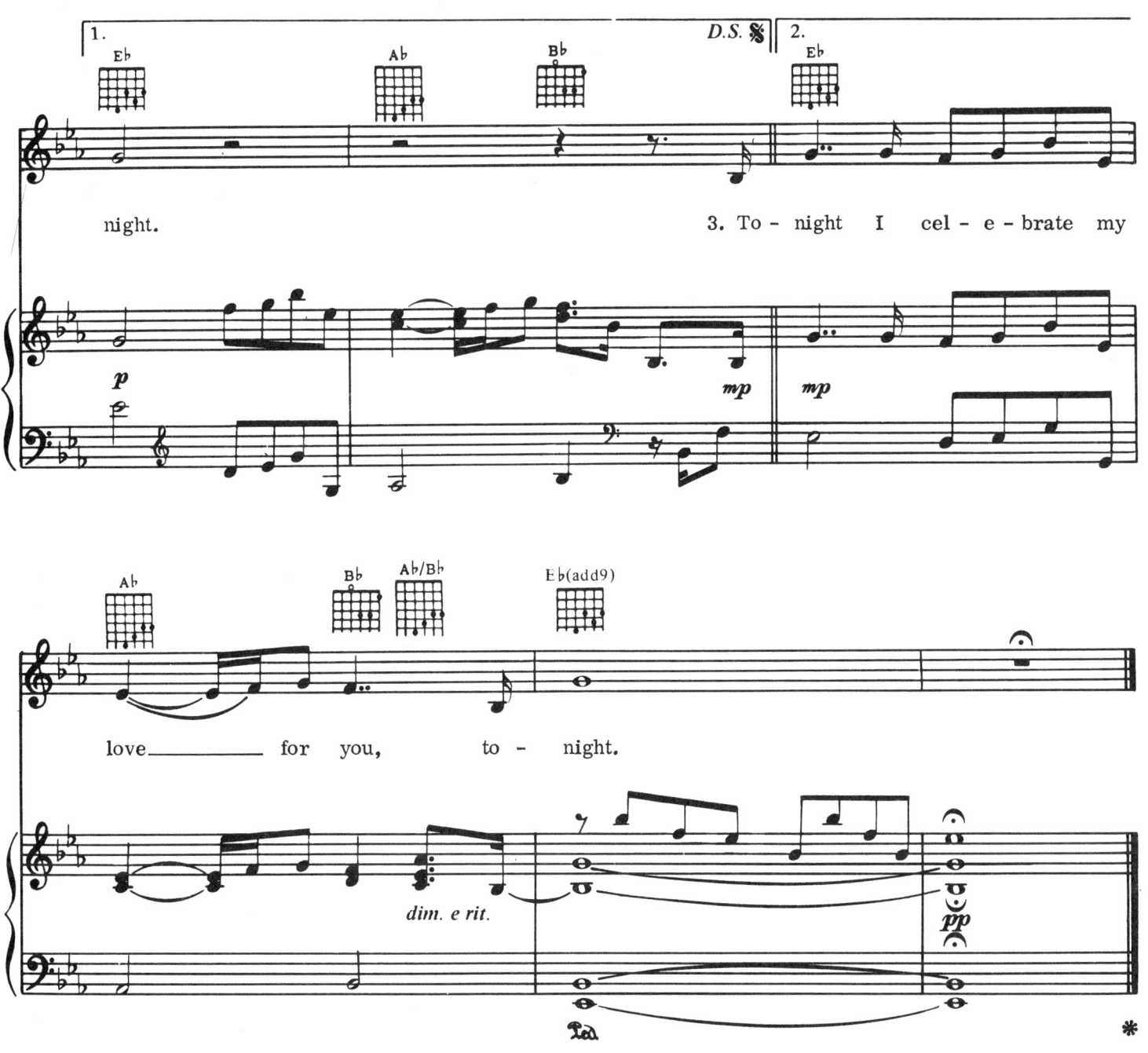

*Verse 3:*
Tonight I celebrate my love for you,
And soon this old world will seem brand new.
Tonight we will both discover
How friends turn into lovers,
When I make love to you.
*(To Chorus:)*

34

The Greatest Love Of All - 5 - 2

# AVE MARIA

(From The First Prelude Of Johann Sebastian Bach)

Adapted by CHARLES GOUNOD

Ave Maria - 4 - 1

Copyright © 1980 by Beam Me Up Music, c/o CPP/BELWIN, INC., Miami, Florida 33014
International Copyright Secured    Made In U.S.A.    All Rights Reserved

42

# BRIDAL CHORUS
(Wedding March From "Lohengrin")

Music by
RICHARD WAGNER

Bridal Chorus - 4 - 1

Copyright © 1978 by BEAM ME UP MUSIC, c/o CPP/BELWIN, INC., Miami, Florida 33014
International Copyright Secured    Made In U.S.A.    All Rights Reserved

46

Bridal Chorus - 4 - 3

Bridal Chorus - 4 - 4

*Verse 3:*
Just you and I;
We care and trust each other.
With you in my life,
There'll never be another.
We'll be all right,
Just you and I.
*(To Chorus:)*

*Verse 2:*
Some hang on to "used-to-be",
Live their lives looking behind.
All we have is here and now;
All our life, out there to find.
The road is long.
There are mountains in our way,
But we climb them a step every day.

# I HONESTLY LOVE YOU

Words and Music by
PETER ALLEN and
JEFF BARRY

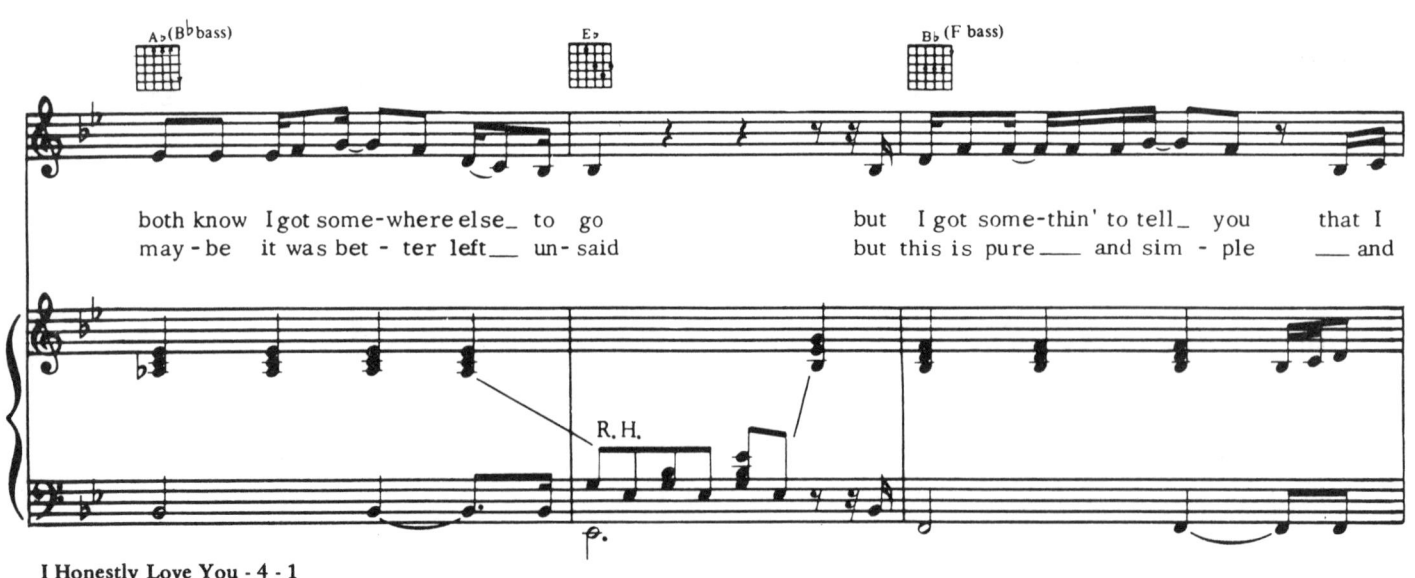

# HEAVEN

Words and Music by
BRYAN ADAMS and
JIM VALLANCE

Slow Rock ♩ = 66

*mp*

*with pedal*

**C**     **Am7**     **G**

1. Oh, think-in' a-bout all our young-er years; there was
2. Oh, once in your life you will find some-one who will

**Dm**     **Am**     **B♭add2**     **Gsus**     **G**

on-ly you and me; we were young and wild and free.
turn your world a-round; bring you up when you're feel-ing down.

Heaven - 4 - 1

Copyright © 1984 IRVING MUSIC, INC. (BMI), CALYPSO TOONZ and ADAMS COMMUNICATIONS (PROC)
International Copyright Secured     Made In U.S.A.     All Rights Reserved

I'm not a-lone an-y-more. For once I can say this is mine, you can't take it, Long as I know I have love, I can make it, For Once In My Life I have some-one who needs me. For once I can feel that some-bod-y's heard my plea, For Once In My Life I have some-one who needs me.

From The Vestron Motion Picture "Dirty Dancing"

# (I'VE HAD) THE TIME OF MY LIFE

Words and Music by
FRANKE PREVITE, DONALD MARKOWITZ
and JOHN DeNICOLA

1. I've been waiting for so long, now I've fi-n'lly found some-one to stand by

me. We saw the writ-ing on the wall as we

felt this mag-i-cal fan-ta-sy. Now with

(I've Had) The Time Of My Life - 4 - 1

Copyright © 1987 Knockout Music, Inc., Donald Jay Music, Ltd.,
R.U. Cyrius Music and Dee Anthony Music
International Copyright Secured    Made In U.S.A.    All Rights Reserved

(I've Had) The Time Of My Life - 4 - 3

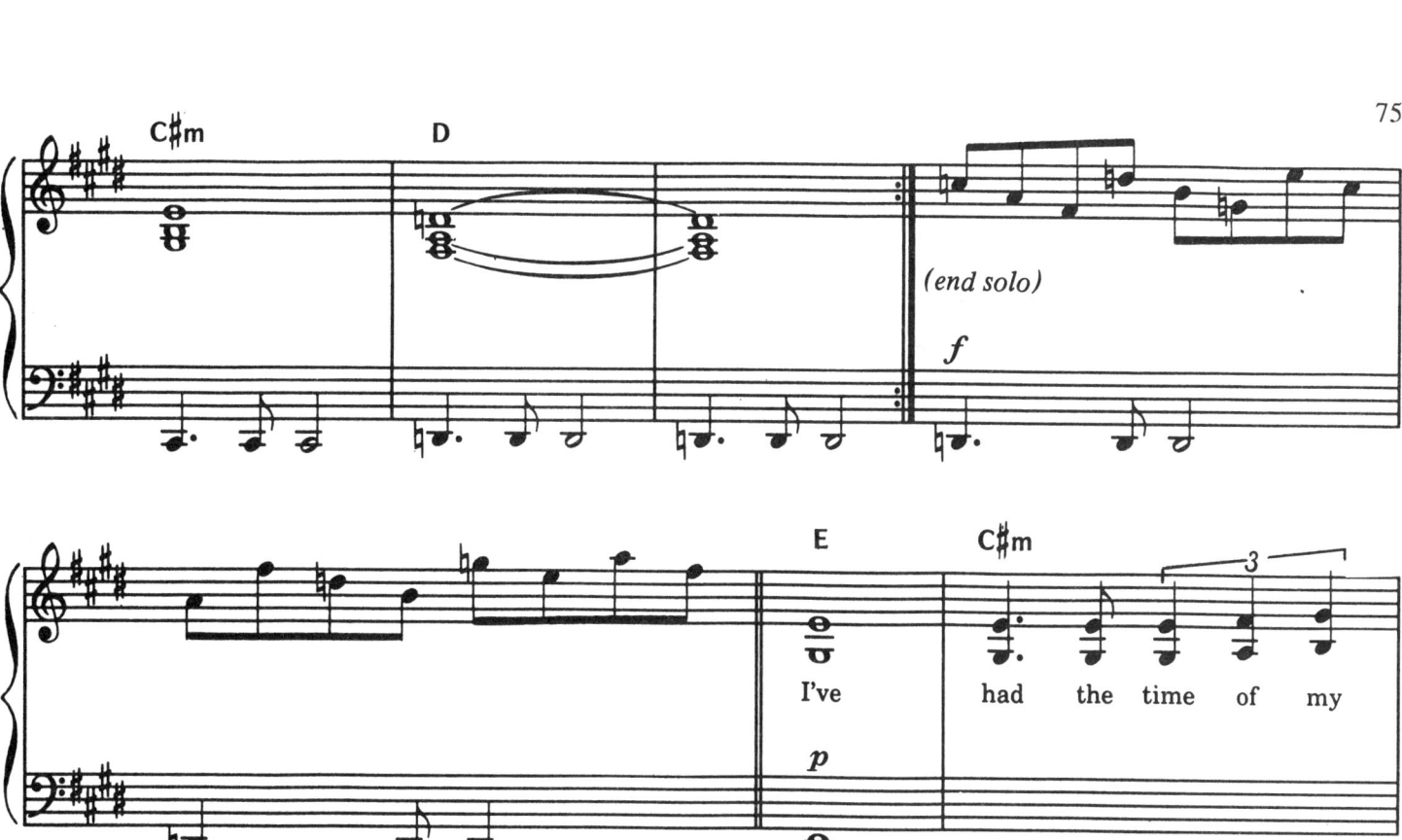

*Verse 2:*
With my body and soul
I want you more than you'll ever know.
So we'll just let it go,
Don't be afraid to lose control.
Yes, I know what's on your mind
When you say, "Stay with me tonight."
Just remember . . .

# THE WEDDING MARCH
(From "Midsummer Night's Dream")

Music by
FELIX MENDELSSOHN

The Wedding March - 2 - 1

Copyright © 1977 ALMO MUSIC CORP. (ASCAP)
International Copyright Secured     Made In U.S.A.     All Rights Reserved

# FOREVER AND EVER, AMEN

Words and Music by
DON SCHLITZ and
PAUL OVERSTREET

Forever And Ever, Amen - 4 - 1

Copyright © 1987 WRITERS GROUP MUSIC/SCARLET MOON MUSIC AND
MCA MUSIC, A DIV. OF MCA, INC./DON SCHLITZ MUSIC
International Copyright Secured     Made In U.S.A.     All Rights Reserved

Chorus:

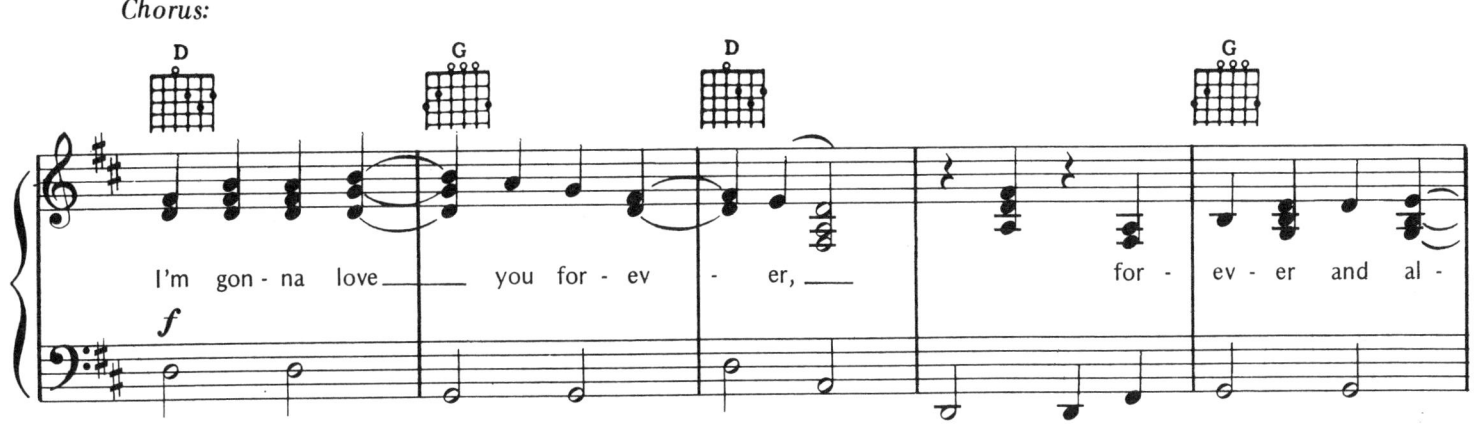

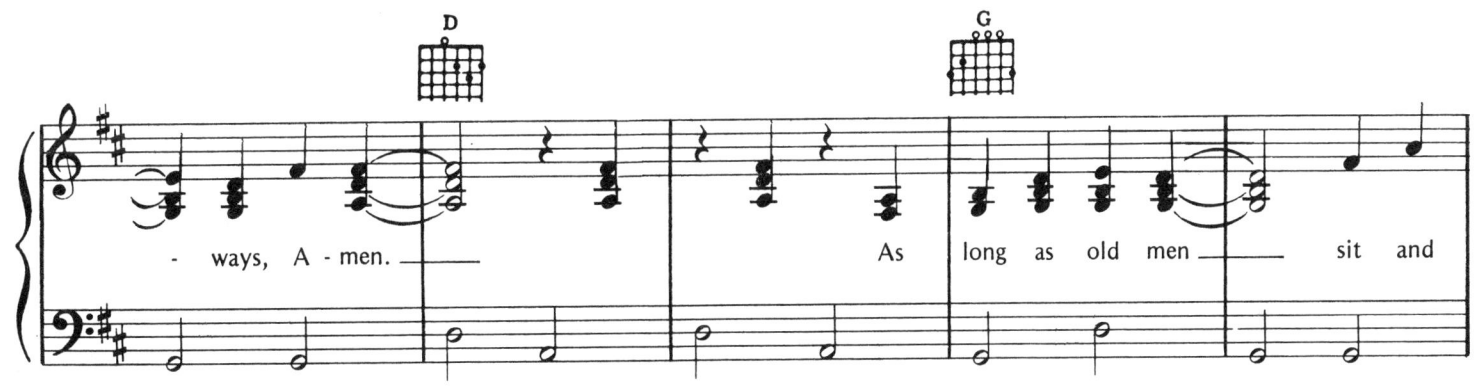

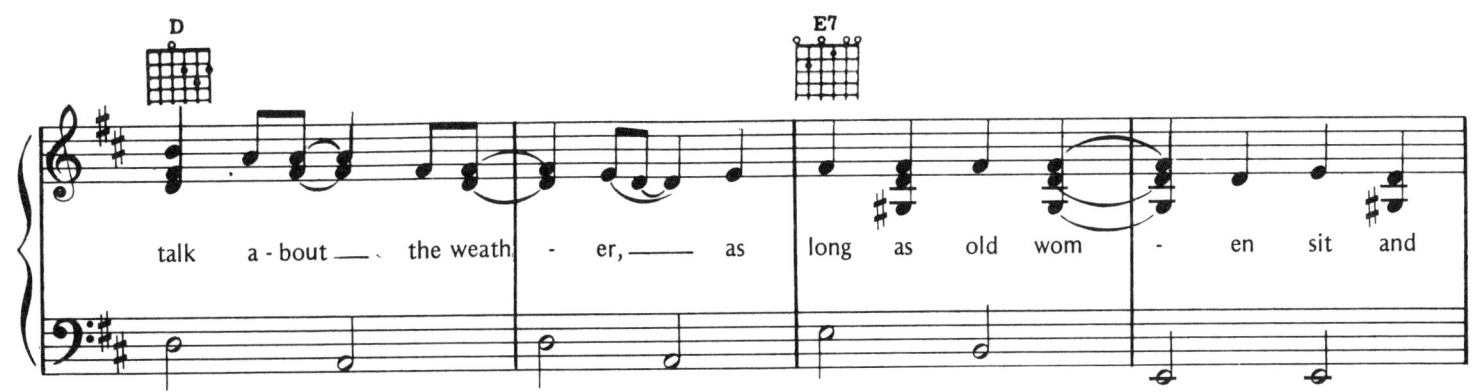

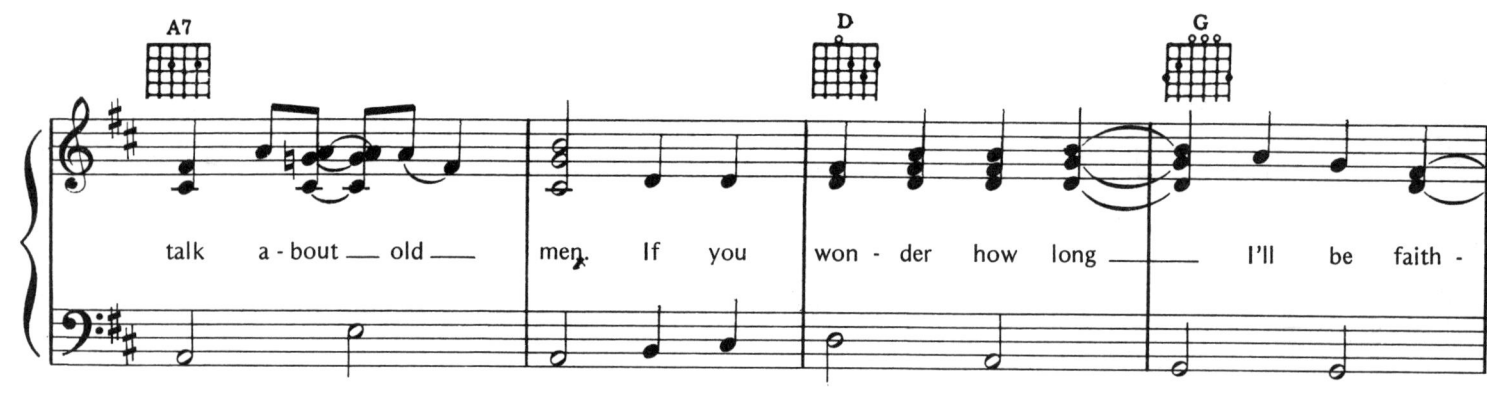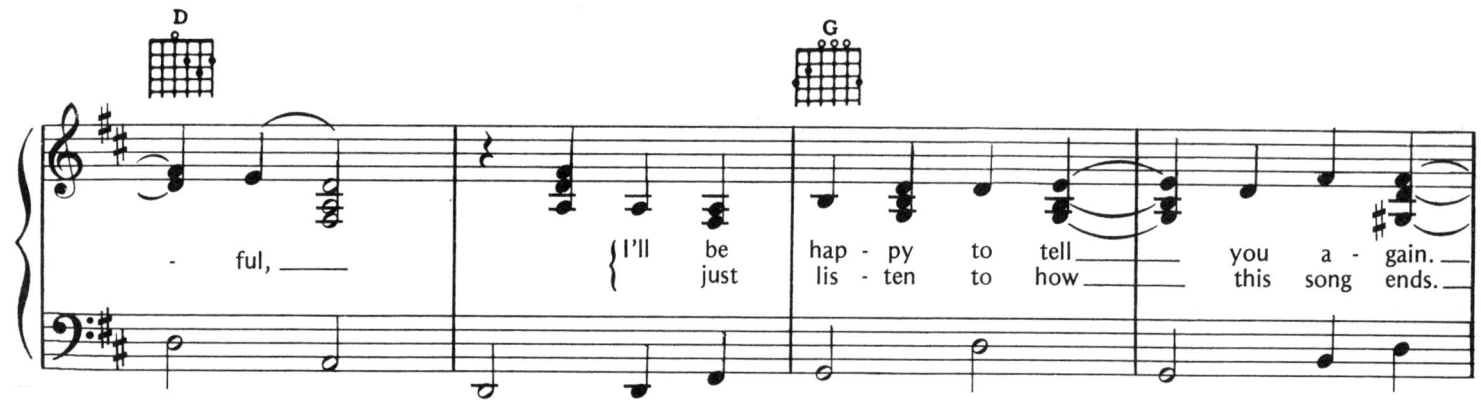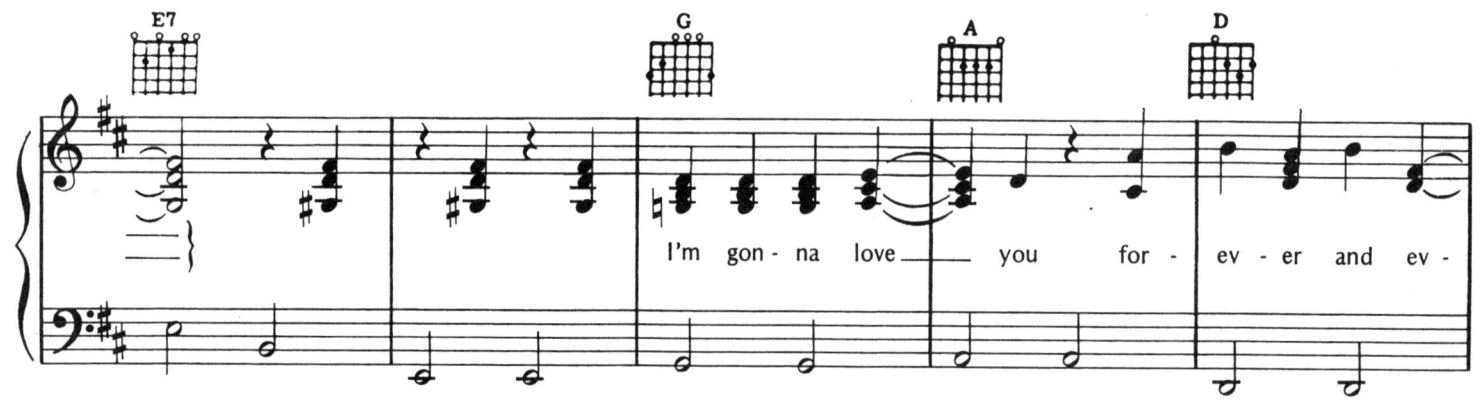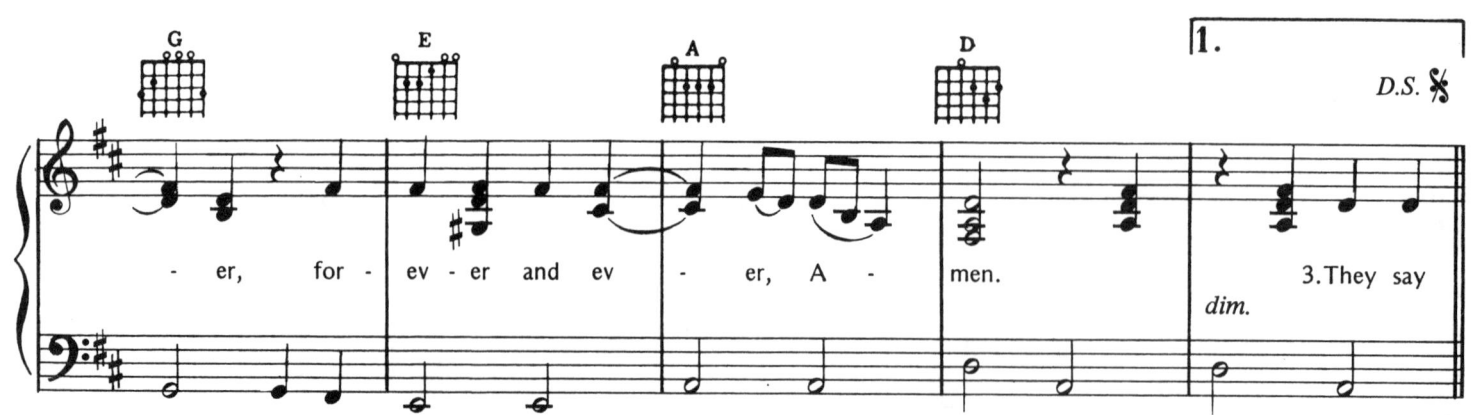

Forever And Ever, Amen - 4 - 3

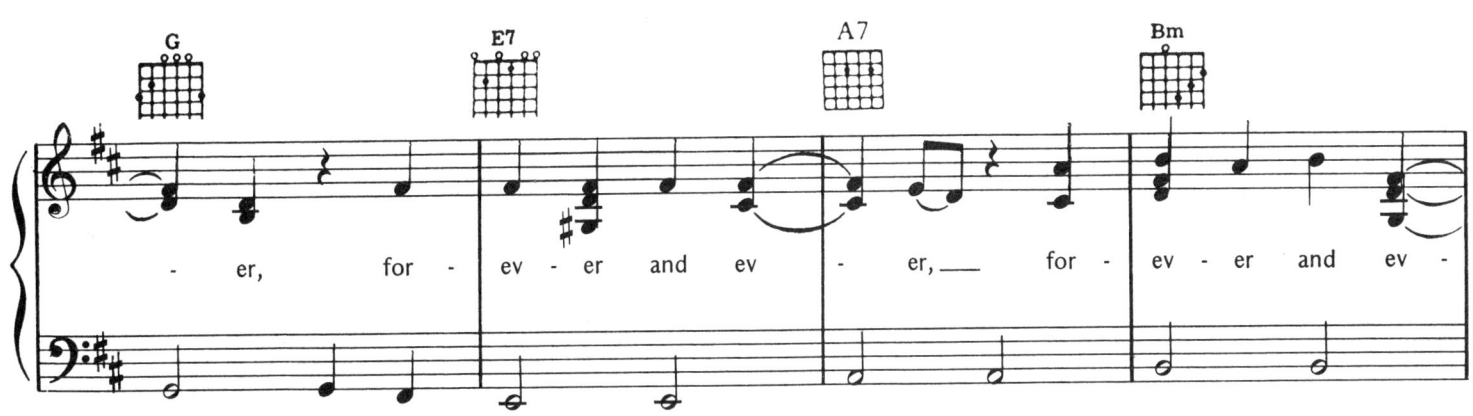
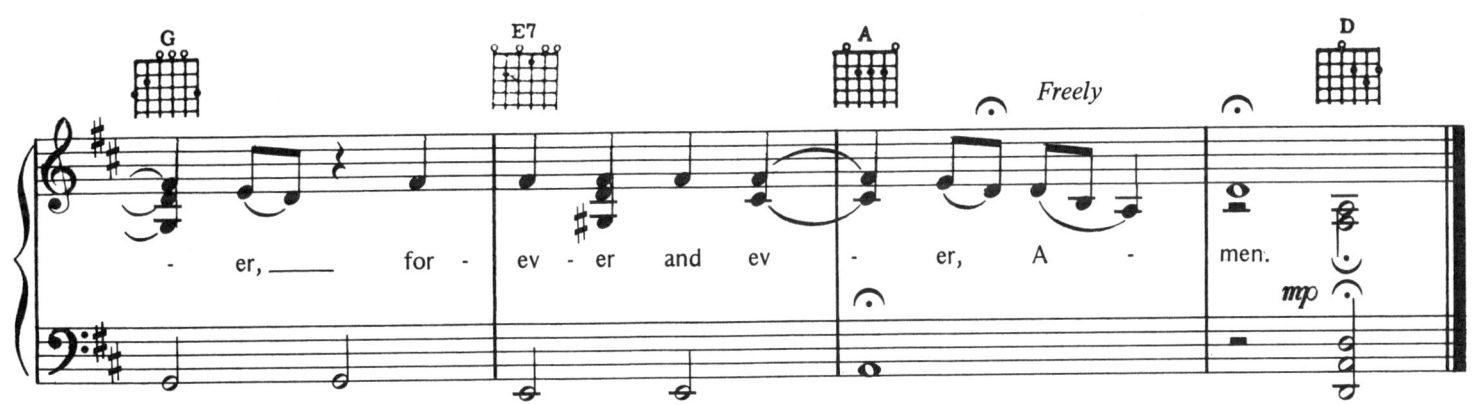

*Verse 2:*
You're not just time that I'm killing.
I'm no longer one of those guys.
As sure as I live, this love that I give
Is gonna be yours until the day that I die.
*(To Chorus:)*

*Verse 3:*
They say time takes its toll on a body,
Makes a young girl's brown hair turn gray.
Well, honey I don't care. I ain't in love with your hair.
And if it all fell out I'd love you any way.

*Verse 4:*
Well, they say time can play tricks on a memory,
Make people forget things they knew.
Well it's easy to see it's happening to me.
I've already forgotten every woman but you.
*(To Chorus:)*

Feelings - 5 - 5

# IF YOU SAY MY EYES ARE BEAUTIFUL

Words and Music by
ELLIOT WILLENSKY

*Verse 2:*
Bitter sweet memories, that's all I have and all I'm taking with me.
Good-bye, oh please don't cry, 'cause we both know that I'm not what you need, but . . .
*(To Chorus:)*

*Verse 3: (Recite)*
And I hope life will treat you kind, and I hope that you have all that you ever dreamed of.
Oh, I do wish you joy, and I wish you happiness, but above all this, I wish you love;
*I love you, I will always love you. (To Chorus:)*

# AND I LOVE YOU SO

Words and Music by
DON McLEAN

Moderately slow

1.-3. And I love you so,
2. And you love me too,

The people ask me how,
Your thoughts are just for me,

How I've lived till now,
You set my spirit free,

*To Coda*

I tell them I don't know.
I'm happy that you do.

I guess they understand,
The book of life is brief,

Copyright © 1970 MAYDAY MUSIC, INC., a division of MERIT MUSIC CORP. and THE BENNY BIRD CO.
International Copyright Secured    Made In U.S.A.    All Rights Reserved

# AVE MARIA

FRANZ SCHUBERT, Op. 52

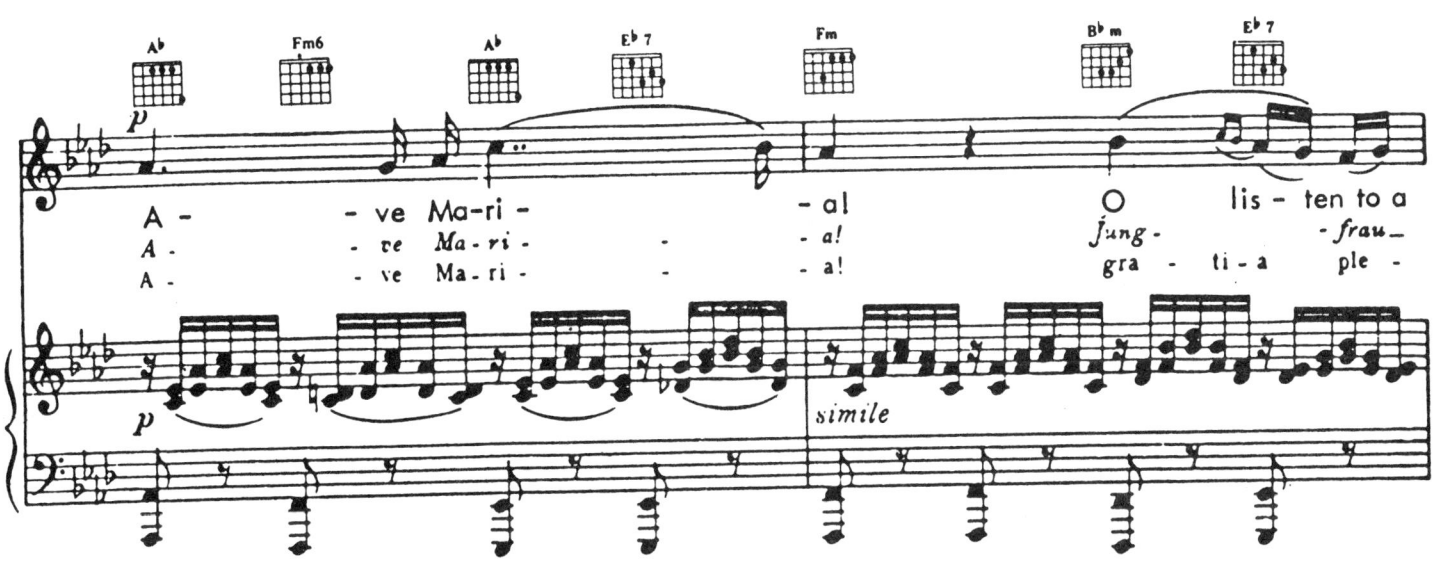

Ave Maria - 7 - 1

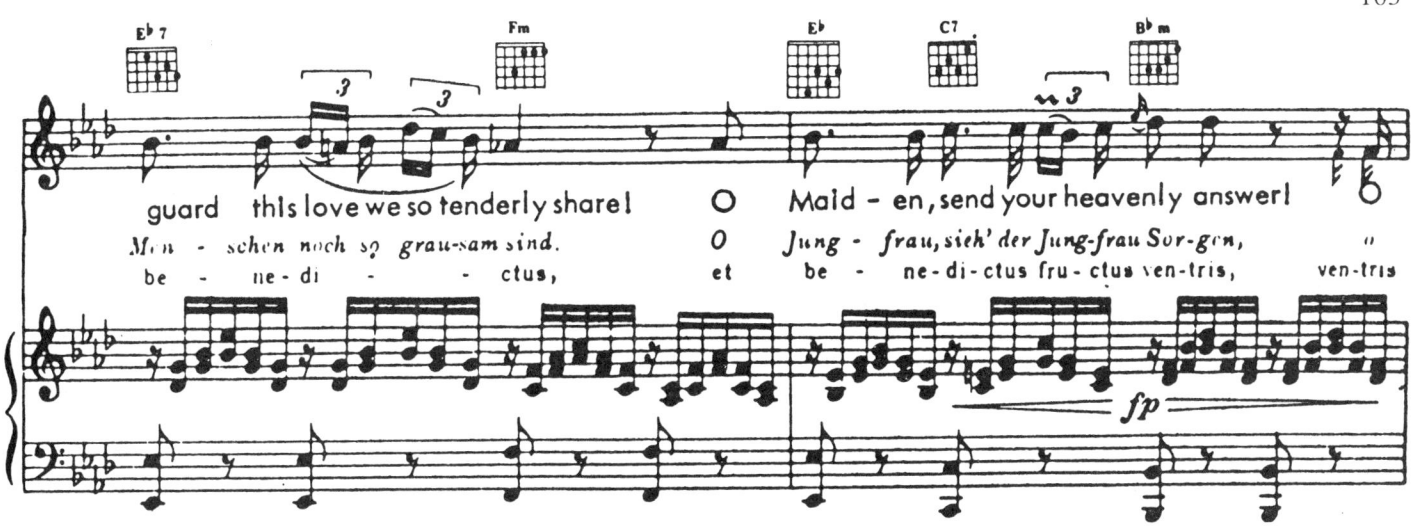

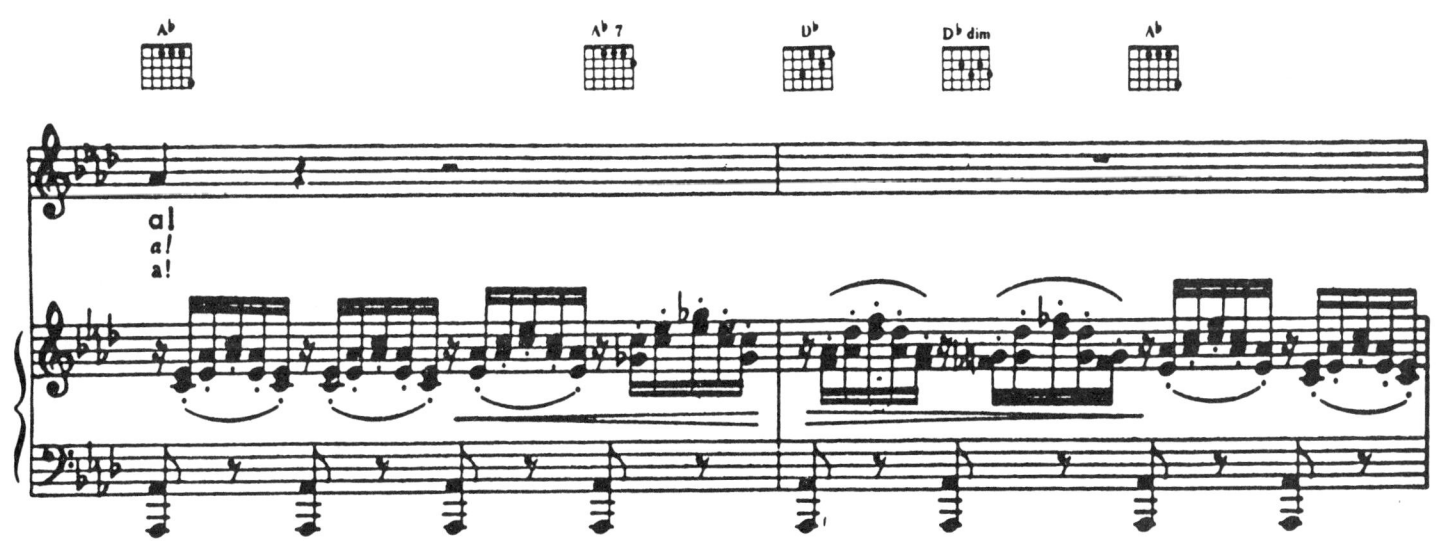

104

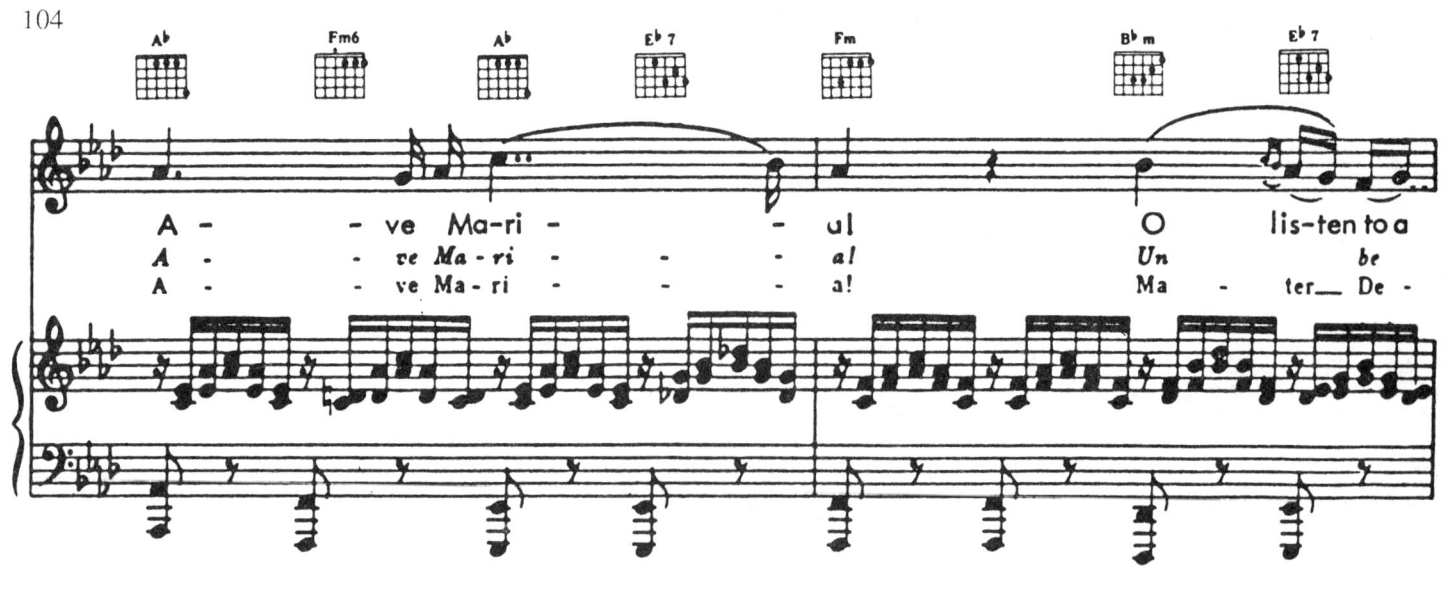

Ave Maria - 7 - 4

*Verse 2:*
You look at me and I begin to melt
Just like the snow, when a ray of sun is felt.
And I'm crazy 'bout you, baby, can't you see?
I'd be so delighted if you would come with me.
*(To Chorus:)*

123

# YOU AND ME AGAINST THE WORLD

Words and Music by
PAUL WILLIAMS and
KEN ASCHER

You and me ___ a-gainst the world ___ some-times it feels like you and me ___ a-gainst the world ___ when all the oth-ers turn their back ___ and walk a-way ___ you ___ can count on me to stay. Re-mem-ber when the

You And Me Against The World - 5 - 1

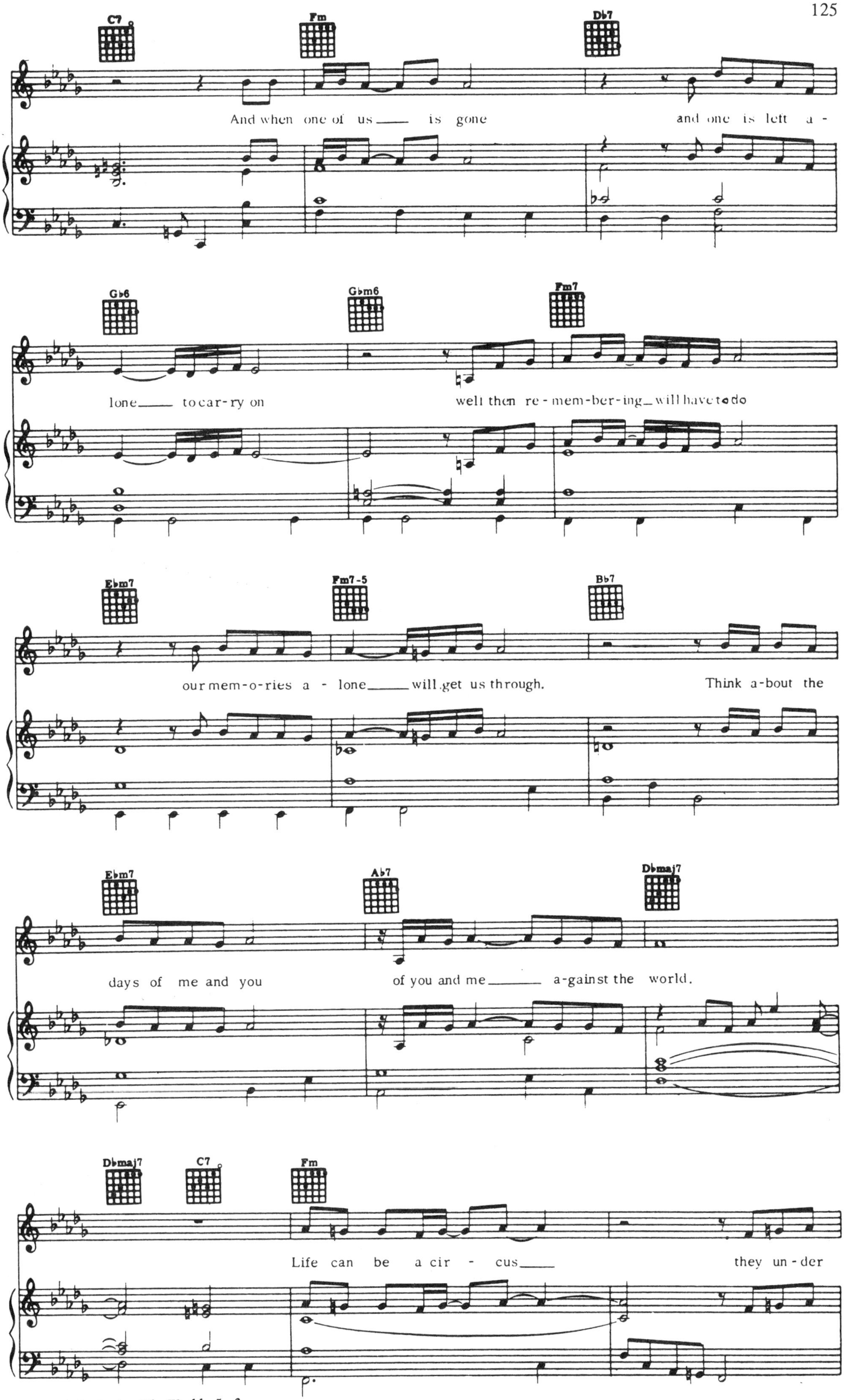
C7 Fm Db7
And when one of us is gone and one is left a -
Gb6 Gbm6 Fm7
lone to car-ry on well then re-mem-ber-ing will have to do
Ebm7 Fm7-5 Bb7
our mem-o-ries a - lone will get us through. Think a-bout the
Ebm7 Ab7 Dbmaj7
days of me and you of you and me a-gainst the world.
Dbmaj7 C7 Fm
Life can be a cir - cus they un-der

# YOU ARE SO BEAUTIFUL

Words and Music by
BILLY PRESTON and
BRUCE FISHER

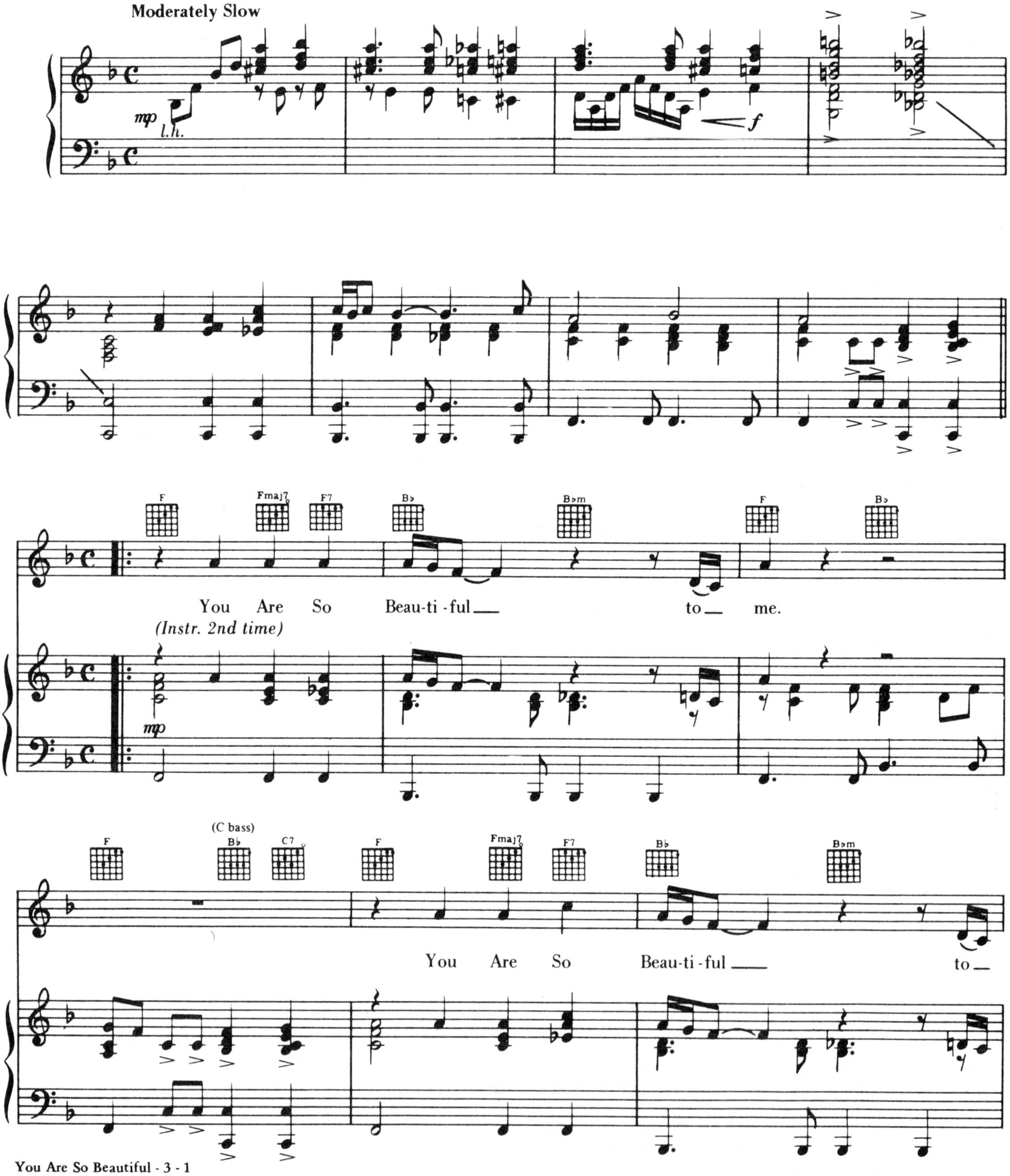

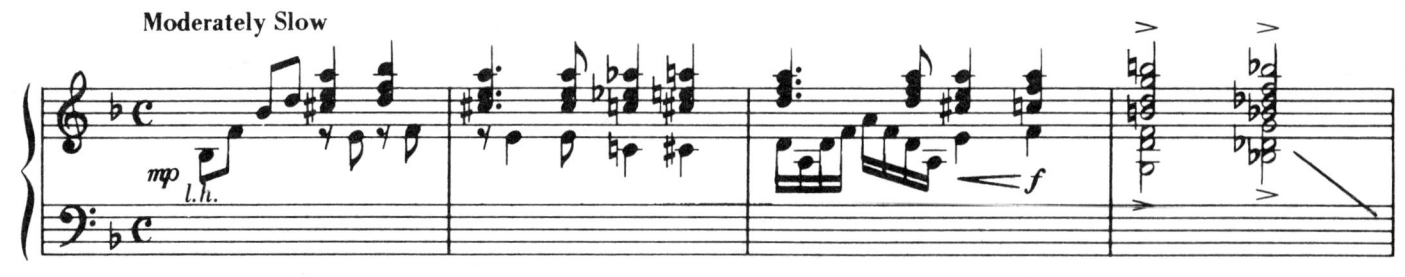

You Are So Beautiful - 3 - 3

*%* Verse 2:
And I know (yes, I know)
That it's plain to see
We're so in love when we're together.
Now I know (now I know)
That I need you here with me
From tonight until the end of time.
You should know everywhere I go;
Always on my mind, you're in my heart, in my soul.

(To Chorus:)

137

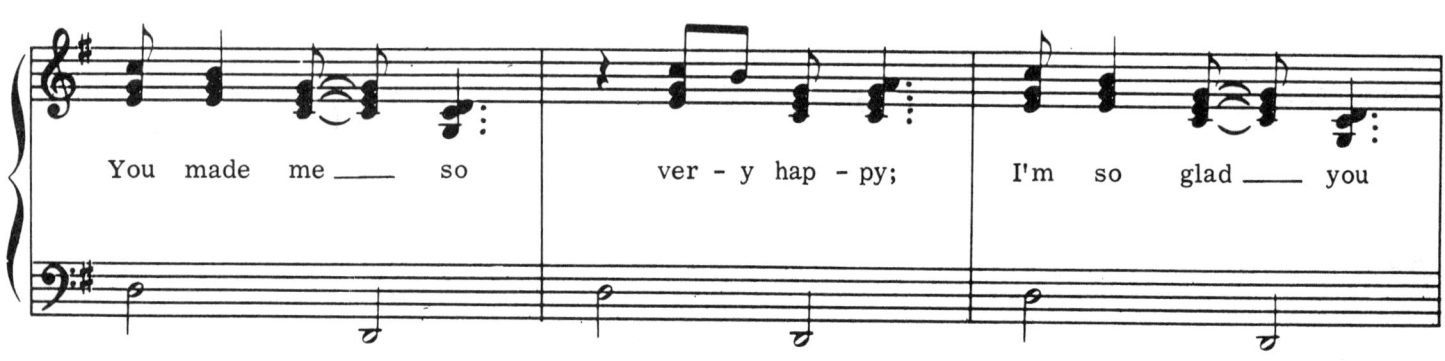

2. The others were untrue, but when it came to you,
   I'd spend my whole life with you.
   'Cause you came and took control,
   You touched my very soul.
   You always showed me that loving you was where it's at.

Verse 3:
You'll keep me standing tall;
You'll help me through it all.
I'm always strong when you're beside me.
I have always needed you;
I could never make it alone.
*(To Chorus:)*

The Shadow Of Your Smile - 2 - 2

Always And Forever - 3 - 2

Always And Forever - 3 - 3

*Verse 2:*
Darlin', inside your eyes, I can see mysteries there.
And you're melting the ice surrounding me;
I'm no longer scared.
I feel you inside my soul, and I'm captured tonight.
But don't let go; this is paradise. *(To Chorus:)*

*Verse 3:*
I feel you inside my soul, and I'm captured tonight.
But don't let go; this is paradise. *(To Chorus:)*

*Verse 3:*
No summer's high; no warm July;
No harvest moon to light one tender August night.
No autumn breeze; no falling leaves;
Not even time for birds to fly to southern skies.

*Verse 4:*
No Libra sun; no Halloween;
No giving thanks to all the Christmas joy you bring.
But what it is, though old so new
To fill your heart like no three words could ever do.

*(To Chorus:)*

151

# ALWAYS AND FOREVER

Words and Music by
ROD TEMPERTON

Always And Forever - 3 - 1

Copyright © 1976 RONDOR MUSIC (LONDON) LTD.
All rights administered in U.S.A. and Canada by ALMO MUSIC CORP. (ASCAP)
This arrangement Copyright © 1978 RONDOR MUSIC (LONDON) LTD.
International Copyright Secured    Made In U.S.A.    All Rights Reserved

*Verse 2:*
Darlin', inside your eyes, I can see mysteries there.
And you're melting the ice surrounding me;
I'm no longer scared.
I feel you inside my soul, and I'm captured tonight.
But don't let go; this is paradise. *(To Chorus:)*

*Verse 3:*
I feel you inside my soul, and I'm captured tonight.
But don't let go; this is paradise. *(To Chorus:)*

# I JUST CALLED TO SAY I LOVE YOU

Words and Music by
STEVIE WONDER

I Just Called To Say I Love You - 5 - 1

Copyright © 1984 JOBETE MUSIC CO., INC. and BLACK BULL MUSIC, INC.
International Copyright Secured    Made In U.S.A.    All Rights Reserved

*to give a way.* / *the month of June.* No first of / But what it spring; / is no song to sing. / is some-thing true, In fact here's just an-oth-er or- / made up of these three words that I -di-nar-y day. 2. No A-pril

I Just Called To Say I Love You - 5 - 4

*Verse 3:*
No summer's high; no warm July;
No harvest moon to light one tender August night.
No autumn breeze; no falling leaves;
Not even time for birds to fly to southern skies.

*Verse 4:*
No Libra sun; no Halloween;
No giving thanks to all the Christmas joy you bring.
But what it is, though old so new
To fill your heart like no three words could ever do.

*(To Chorus:)*

# I'D FALL IN LOVE TONIGHT

Words and Music by
NAOMI MARTIN and
MIKE REID

Slowly ♩ = 88

*Vocal sung one octave lower
I'd Fall In Love Tonight - 3 - 1

Copyright © 1985 TOM COLLINS MUSIC CORPORATION and LODGE HALL MUSIC, INC.
International Copyright Secured    Made In U.S.A.    All Rights Reserved

172

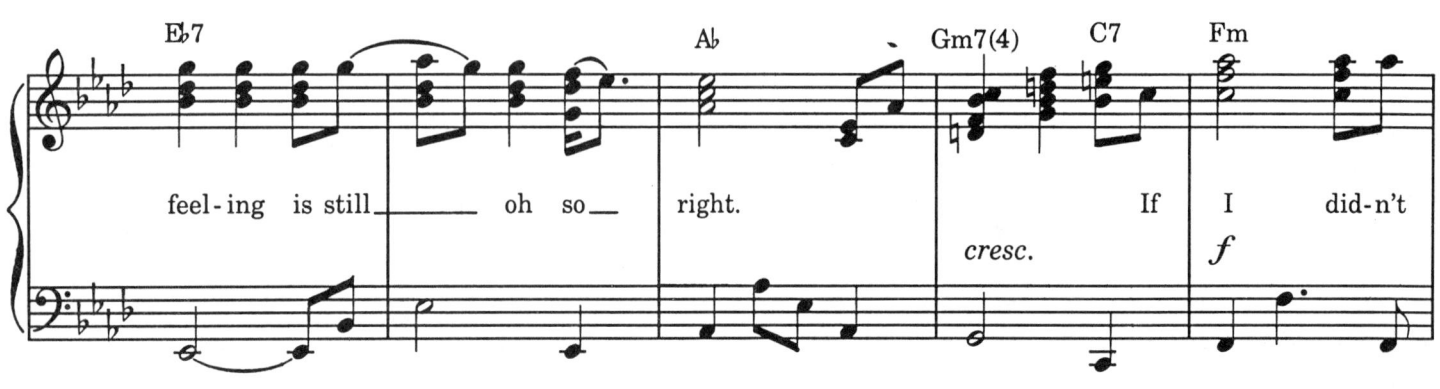

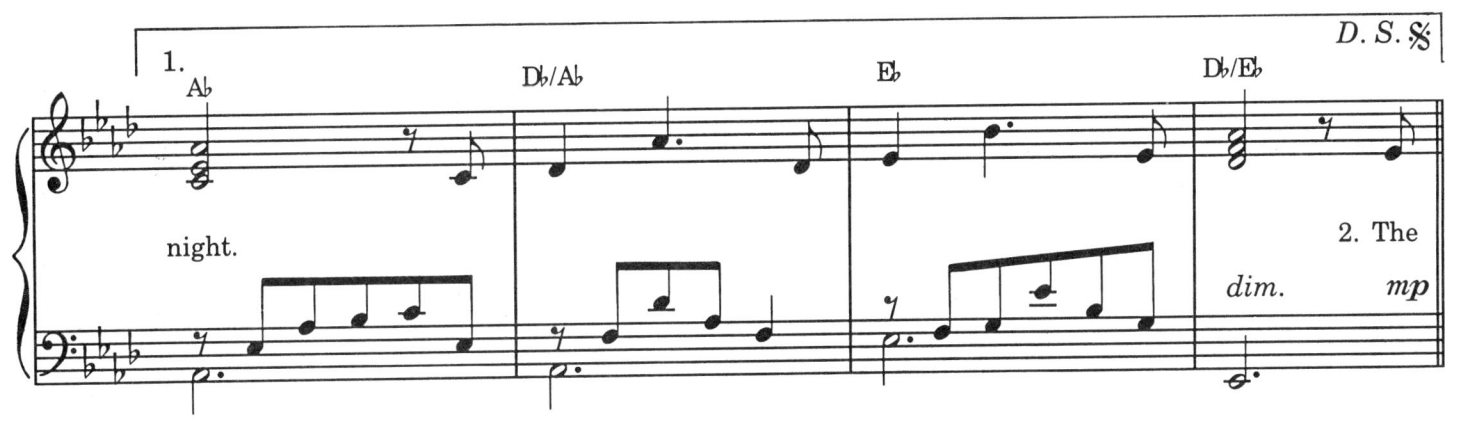
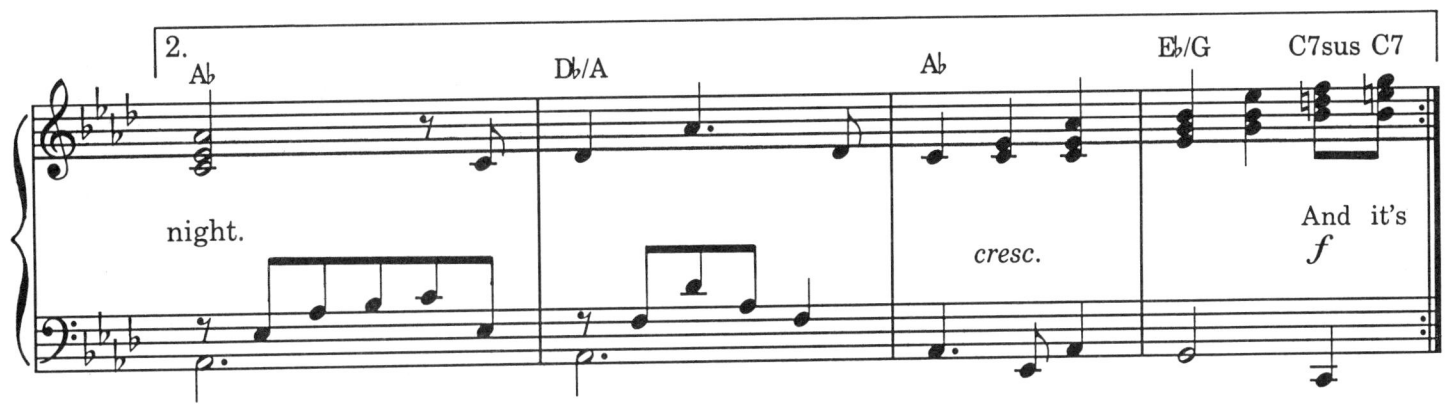
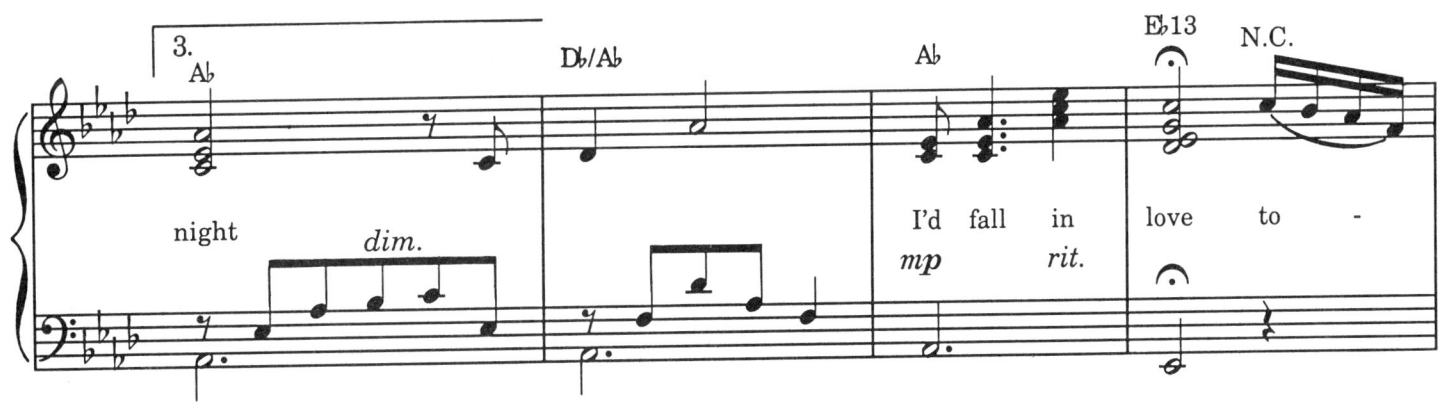

I'd Fall In Love Tonight - 3 - 3

*Verse 2:*
Listen closely to the words I'm sayin',
I know I've never meant them more.
For your love only I've been prayin'.
You and I are what this love is for.

*(To Chorus:)*

# Showstoppers

## Piano/Vocal/Chords:

### 20's, 30's, & 40's SHOWSTOPPERS
(F2865SMX)

100 nostalgic favorites include: Chattanooga Choo Choo • Pennsylvania 6-5000 • Blue Moon • Moonglow • My Blue Heaven • Ain't Misbehavin' • That Old Black Magic and more.

### 50's & 60's SHOWSTOPPERS
(F2864SMA)

Bop back to a simpler time and enjoy: Aquarius/Let The Sunshine In • (Sittin' On) The Dock Of The Bay • Hey, Good Lookin' • Sunny • Johnny Angel and more.

### 70's & 80's SHOWSTOPPERS
(F2863SMC)

Pop songs from two great decades include: Always • The Greatest Love Of All • The Lady In Red • Axel F • Fame • Footloose • You're The Inspiration • Against All Odds (Take A Look At Me Now) and more.

### BROADWAY SHOWSTOPPERS
(F2878SMA)

100 great show tunes include: Ain't Misbehavin' • Almost Like Being In Love • Consider Yourself • Give My Regards To Broadway • Good Morning Starshine • Mood Indigo • Send In The Clowns • Tomorrow.

### CHRISTMAS SHOWSTOPPERS
P/V/C (F2868SMA)
Easy Piano (F2924P2X) / Big Note (F2925P3X)

Trim your tree with these 100 favorite holiday songs, including: Sleigh Ride • Silver Bells • Deck The Halls • Have Yourself A Merry Little Christmas • Here Comes Santa Claus • Little Drummer Boy • Let It Snow! Let It Snow! Let It Snow!

### COUNTRY SHOWSTOPPERS
(F2902SMA)

100 country classics include: Blue Bayou • Dear Me • Forever And Ever, Amen • Don't It Make My Brown Eyes Blue • The Gambler • Kiss An Angel Good Mornin' • Let Me Be There • The Most Beautiful Girl.

### JAZZ SHOWSTOPPERS
(F2953SMX)

101 standard jazz tunes including: Misty • Elmer's Tune • Birth Of The Blues • It Don't Mean A Thing (If It Ain't Got That Swing).

### MOVIE SHOWSTOPPERS
(F2866SMA)

100 songs from memorable motion pictures include: Axel F • Up Where We Belong • Speak Softly Love (from *The Godfather*) • The Entertainer • Fame • Nine To Five • Nobody Does It Better.

### RAGTIME SHOWSTOPPERS
(F2867SMX)

These 100 original classic rags by Scott Joplin, James Scott, Joseph Lamb and other ragtime composers include: Maple Leaf Rag • The Entertainer • Kansas City Rag • Ma Rag Time Baby • The St. Louis Rag • World's Fair Rag and many others.

### ROMANTIC SHOWSTOPPERS
(F2870SMB)

100 lovely melodies include: Always • And I Love You So • The First Time Ever I Saw Your Face • The Lady In Red • Moonglow • Somewhere, My Love • (I've Had) The Time Of My Life • Weekend In New England • A Time For Us (Love Theme from *Romeo And Juliet*).

### TELEVISION SHOWSTOPPERS
(F2874SMB)

Enjoy 102 themes from TV's current and classic hits: Who's The Boss • Dallas • Entertainment Tonight • Fame • Masterpiece Theatre • Newhart • Solid Gold • Star Trek • St. Elsewhere • The Odd Couple and more.

## Big Note Piano:

### BIG NOTE PIANO SHOWSTOPPERS
Vol. 1 (F2871P3B) / Vol. 2 (F2918P3A)

Easy-to-read big note arrangements of 100 popular tunes include: (They Long To Be) Close To You • Do You Want To Know A Secret? • If Ever You're In My Arms Again • Moon River • Over The Rainbow • Singin' In The Rain • You Light Up My Life • Theme From *Love Story*.

## Easy Piano:

### EASY PIANO SHOWSTOPPERS
Vol. 1 (F2875P2B) / Vol. 2 (F2912P2A)

100 easy piano arrangements of familiar songs include: Alfie • Baby Elephant Walk • Classical Gas • Don't Cry Out Loud • Colour My World • The Pink Panther • I Honestly Love You • Raindrops Keep Fallin' On My Head.

## Easy Organ:

### EASY ORGAN SHOWSTOPPERS
(F2873EOA)

100 great current hits and timeless standards in easy arrangements for organ include: After The Lovin' • Always And Forever • Come Saturday Morning • I Just Called To Say I Love You • Isn't She Lovely • On The Wings Of Love • Up Where We Belong • You Light Up My Life.

## Intermediate Piano Solos:

### CLASSICAL PIANO SHOWSTOPPERS
(F2872P9X)

100 classical piano solos include: Arioso • Bridal Chorus (from *Lohengrin*) • Clair De Lune • Fifth Symphony (Theme) • Minuet In G • Moonlight Sonata (1st Movement) • Polovetsian Dance (from *Prince Igor*) • The Swan • Wedding March (from *A Midsummer Night's Dream*).

### POPULAR PIANO SHOWSTOPPERS
(F2876P9A)

100 popular piano solos include: Baby Elephant Walk • Gonna Fly Now (Theme from *Rocky*) • The Hill Street Blues Theme • Love Is A Many-Splendored Thing • (Love Theme from) *Romeo And Juliet* • Separate Lives (Love Theme from *White Nights*) • The Shadow Of Your Smile • Theme From *The Apartment* • From *New York, New York*.